The Great Book
of Oriental Carpets

E. Gans-Ruedin

The Great Book of Oriental Carpets

1817

HARPER & ROW, PUBLISHERS, New York

Cambridge, Philadelphia, San Francisco,
London, Mexico City, Sao Paulo, Sydney

Photo Credits

The photographs in this book are the work of
René Bersier: 1–33, 35–36, 38–41, 47–48, 53, 57–59, 64–70, 80
Leo Hilber: 34, 37, 42–46, 49–52, 54–56, 60–63, 71–79
Drawings by Jean-Paul Chablais and Walter Hugentobler

Translated from the French, *Beauté du Tapis d'Orient* by Valerie Howard
English translation © 1983 by Office du Livre, Fribourg, Switzerland

First published in English in 1983
by Harper & Row Publishers, Inc.
10 East 53rd Street
New York, New York 10022
© 1983 Office du Livre, Fribourg, Switzerland

First U.S. Edition

ISBN: 0-06-015194-3
LIBRARY OF CONGRESS CATALOG CARD
NUMBER: 83-47531

83 84 85 86 87 10 9 8 7 6 5 4 3 2 1

Printed and bound in Switzerland

CONTENTS

Most of the books devoted to the Oriental carpet illustrate examples preserved in museums and important collections; the keen collector will consult these to good purpose to widen his knowledge. This volume, however, has a different purpose—that of presenting carpets from the principal areas in the East that are to be found today in the trade and that date from the nineteenth and twentieth centuries. The reproductions are preceded by explanatory and historical notes on the characteristics of the different groups of carpets: the origins of the patterns, the materials, looms and knots.

The name "Oriental carpet" is given in general to all hand-knotted carpets. This denomination is not inexact in view of their common Asiatic origin; however, the immensity of the producing areas and the variety of techniques, styles and materials used necessitate a more detailed classification. As a rule, Oriental carpets are divided into four groups: Turkish or Anatolian rugs, rugs from Persia or Iran, rugs from the Caucasus, and finally rugs from Central Asia or Turkestan, to which one must add those from Afghanistan, India and China. Even in these distant regions, exclusively commercial criteria direct the manufacture, so that the art of rug-making has become truly industrialized.

In China and India, the early production drew to a close in the eighteenth century. Today attempts are being made in India and China to re-establish the old methods of carpet-making. Although carpets from India, Kashmir and China are less familiar in the West than Turkish, Persian or Caucasian examples, their production has greatly increased in recent years following the huge rise in the price of Iranian carpets. The skill and excellence of the craftsmen of the aforementioned countries have enabled them at present to improve considerably the variety of their products by reproducing some designs of Middle Eastern inspiration.

MAJOR CARPET-PRODUCING REGIONS OF THE EAST

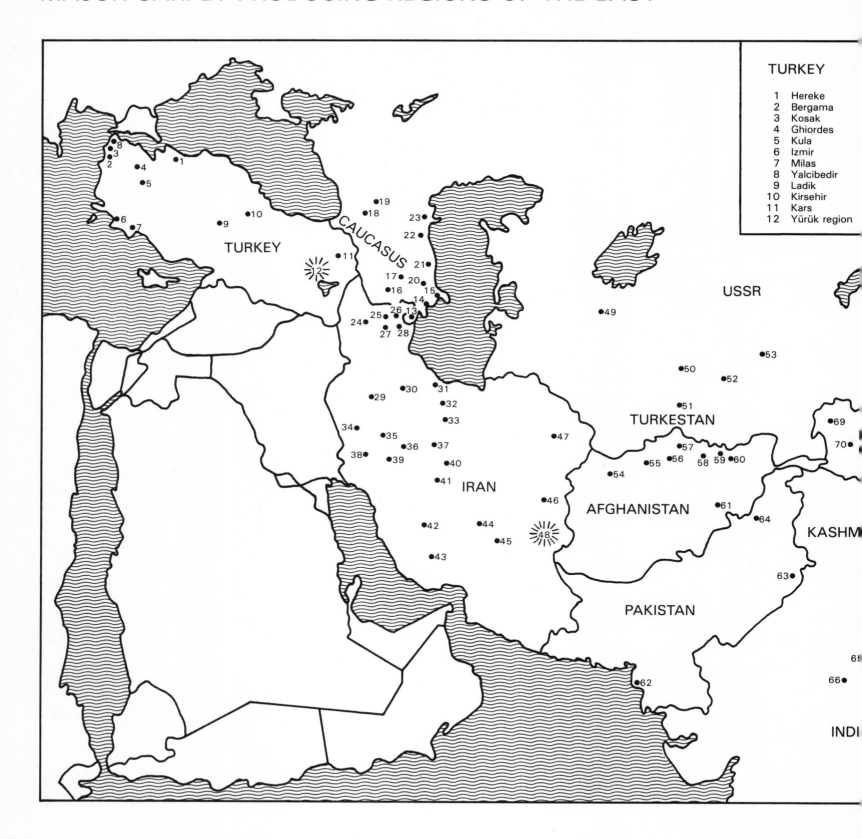

TURKEY

1 Hereke
2 Bergama
3 Kosak
4 Ghiordes
5 Kula
6 Izmir
7 Milas
8 Yalcibedir
9 Ladik
10 Kirsehir
11 Kars
12 Yürük region

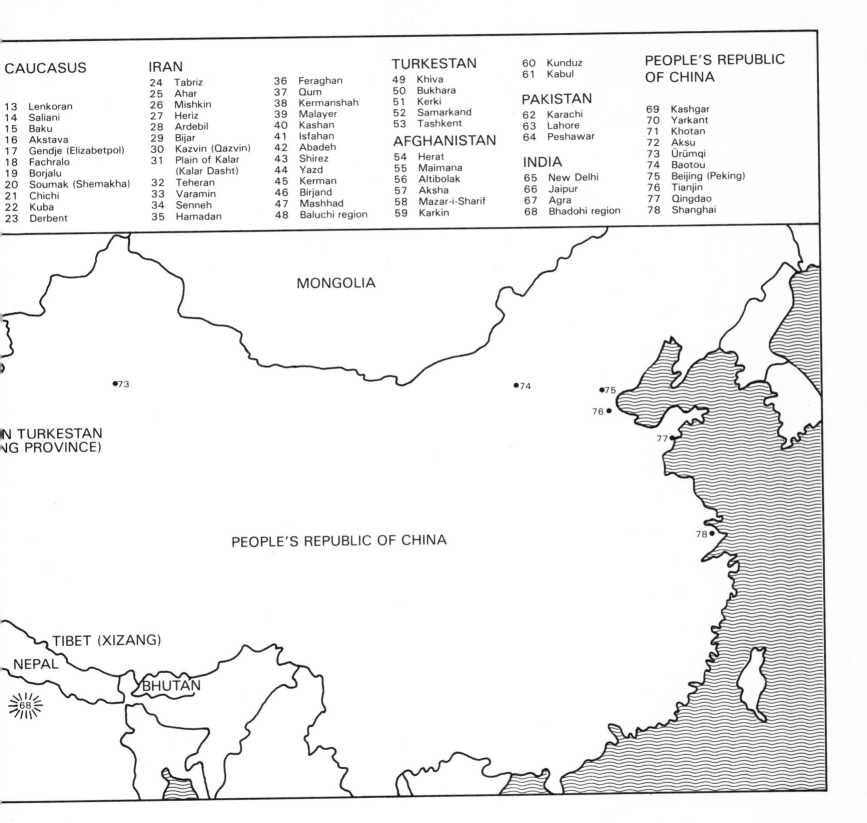

CAUCASUS

13 Lenkoran
14 Saliani
15 Baku
16 Akstava
17 Gendje (Elizabetpol)
18 Fachralo
19 Borjalu
20 Soumak (Shemakha)
21 Chichi
22 Kuba
23 Derbent

IRAN

24 Tabriz
25 Ahar
26 Mishkin
27 Heriz
28 Ardebil
29 Bijar
30 Kazvin (Qazvin)
31 Plain of Kalar
   (Kalar Dasht)
32 Teheran
33 Varamin
34 Senneh
35 Hamadan

36 Feraghan
37 Qum
38 Kermanshah
39 Malayer
40 Kashan
41 Isfahan
42 Abadeh
43 Shirez
44 Yazd
45 Kerman
46 Birjand
47 Mashhad
48 Baluchi region

TURKESTAN

49 Khiva
50 Bukhara
51 Kerki
52 Samarkand
53 Tashkent

AFGHANISTAN

54 Herat
55 Maimana
56 Altibolak
57 Aksha
58 Mazar-i-Sharif
59 Karkin

60 Kunduz
61 Kabul

PAKISTAN

62 Karachi
63 Lahore
64 Peshawar

INDIA

65 New Delhi
66 Jaipur
67 Agra
68 Bhadohi region

PEOPLE'S REPUBLIC OF CHINA

69 Kashgar
70 Yarkant
71 Khotan
72 Aksu
73 Ürümqi
74 Baotou
75 Beijing (Peking)
76 Tianjin
77 Qingdao
78 Shanghai

MONGOLIA

●73

●74

●75

76 ●

N TURKESTAN
NG PROVINCE)

77 ●

PEOPLE'S REPUBLIC OF CHINA

78 ●

TIBET (XIZANG)

NEPAL

BHUTAN

68

INTRODUCTION

Historical Notes

Of all objects of furnishing, the carpet is surely the most perishable. Dampness, moths and wear soon take their toll, and so it is only by a miracle that early examples have come down to us.

Carpet-making goes back to the earliest days and is assumed to have originated among the nomadic peoples of Central Asia. Obviously the rug is valued by nomads, as it is such an easily transportable furnishing. Moreover, the pastoral people, to whom wool was one of the main currencies, sought to derive from it the greatest possible advantage, and the sale of ready-made articles assured them of the best return.

The earliest carpet in the world dates from the fifth century B.C. and is in the Hermitage Museum in Leningrad. Preserved in the ice of a Scythian burial mound, it was discovered at Pasyryk in southern Siberia but was probably made in the Iranian highlands. Its technical and artistic perfection is comparable with that of present-day examples. Discoveries made in other Scythian graves make it clear that the art of knotting was so perfect that it has hardly progressed since antiquity: the Turkish and the Persian knot were already in existence, and the high quality of the construction yields nothing to present-day products.

We have only the scantiest information on the period from the fifth century B.C. to the twelfth century A.D. In the ninth century, Turkoman hordes from Central Asia invaded the whole of the Middle East as far as Turkey. The diffusion of the art of carpet-knotting in all of the countries which they annexed owes much to them. The Seljuk dynasty established by them in Turkey encouraged the fine arts, and carpet manufacture enjoyed a long period of prosperity.

Rugs of this period were imported into Europe by the Venetians and are familiar to us mainly through the works of contemporary painters—we talk of the "Lotto" rug and the "Holbein" carpet, as these artists tended to reproduce a particular type of Turkish rug in their canvases. In the sixteenth century, Shah Tahmasp, the second ruler of the Safavid dynasty, united Persia and inspired a veritable renaissance of the decorative arts there. He was himself a practitioner of calligraphy and illumination and had designs for carpets created by miniaturists. It was in this way that the first examples of carpets with a central medallion appeared, reminiscent in design of manuscript covers.

Examples from the period, which are to be found nowadays in museums and private collections, give an accurate idea of their perfection, for these carpets are real jewels of the art, incomparable in the beauty and harmony of their choice of colours and the imagination of their patterns, and executed in the most precious materials, combining silk with wool brocaded with gold and silver.

It was not without reason that Mohammed conceived the Garden of Eden gay with flowers at the summit of a mountain, where a sparkling fountain played, surrounded with seats draped with multicolored rugs. In all of the courts of the East, and especially in Persia, the carpet formed the essential element of the spectacular ostentation of a civilization that combined splendour and fantasy. Sadly much of this beauty was destroyed through war, fire and religious or dynastic conflict. It was under the reign of Shah Abbas the Great (1587 to

1628) that the finest carpets in Persian art were produced in Isfahan, the former capital of Persia. They adorned the palace of the Shah in profusion. At the "International Exhibition of Persian Art" at Burlington House in London in 1931, the catalogue included 135 carpets of the sixteenth and seventeenth centuries lent by the major European and American museums. Even the Museum of the Shrine at Mashhad participated in this exhibition, which was highly successful and contributed to the recognition of the artistry of the Persian carpet.

The arrangement of the typical Oriental house, where furniture is almost unknown, was certainly conducive to the spread of the carpet-making art in the East. Oriental peoples satisfy their insatiable appetite for decoration through ceramics, incised metalwork and, above all, textiles, of which the rug is the most noble illustration, while at the same time being a most practical and comfortable furnishing. This fondness for textiles is still retained today, and Oriental peoples all possess carpets be they large or small. Affection for the carpet is especially strong among nomads, who use it at night to adorn the tent that shelters them. Nor may peasant girls be married until they have shown their skill in carpet-knotting.

As we have said, it seems most likely that the hand-knotted carpet was the creation of the nomadic tribes of Central Asia. Archaeological discoveries made in eastern Turkestan make it possible to establish that the art had become fully developed in the sixth century among Turkoman nomads. Because of their rigorous living conditions, these nomadic peoples limited their output to modestly sized rugs. The nomadic rug-maker had to dismantle his loom whenever the natural elements or the enemy threatened his safety, forcing him to seek a new site. The assembly and dismantling of the loom is a delicate operation, for hundreds of warp threads must be kept in perfect order so that they do not become entangled. Irregularities in the weave—differences between the two selvedges, unevenness in the lines and faults in the pattern—reveal interruptions in the work but at the same demonstrate the authenticity of the carpet.

The Turkoman invasion of the ninth century at least had the merit of spreading carpet-knotting throughout Asia Minor. The Mogul rugs of India, which are among the finest known examples of the sixteenth and seventeenth centuries, were made during the reigns of Akbar, Jahangir and Shah Jahan at Agra, Fathpur, Lahore and Dehli. They are to be found in the museum and palace of Jaipur, in the Österreichisches Museum für angewandte Kunst in Vienna, in the Keir Collection and the Victoria and Albert Museum in London, as well as in the major museums in the United States. Carpets with floral decoration were influenced by the Persian style of the period, for the craftsmen had come from Persia, but Mogul prayer rugs are typically Indian. The lighter and more delicate colouring of these rugs differed from Persian examples, and the knotting of Mogul rugs is the finest possible. The fragment in silk in the Altmann Collection in the Metropolitan Museum of Art, New York, has a knot count of just over 2,516 knots per square inch (3,900,000 per square metre). Mogul rugs in which the pile, warp and weft are of silk are attributed to the reign of Shah Jahan (1628–1658). After a long period of decline, the Indian carpet is now undergoing a highly promising revival.

In China, the art of knotting carpets was already being practised in Antiquity, as is proven by the fragments of knotted carpets from the third century A.D. discovered at Minfeng and Luolan in Xinjiang province. The Chinese carpet is unique in character and totally harmonious in colour and design, the latter being based on the geometric, stylized and naturalistic style of decorative art proper to China. Today there are carpet-producing centres in the major Chinese cities, in Ningxia, at Baotou, in Xinjiang and in Tibet. In Tientsin, Beijing and Shanghai, in addition to classical Chinese rugs, an important production of silk carpets has developed, some of which are of extremely fine quality. China is currently making great efforts to develop her output of knotted carpets, and some Chinese designs now show Persian influence.

Characteristics of Knotted Carpets

Materials

The supple and strong fleece of the indigenous sheep has always been, and will remain, the basic material used in carpet weaving. It is provided by the many flocks that graze on vast, generally arid, regions. In Anatolia, there is a thriving breed of sheep which, even in antiquity, enjoyed a reputation for the fineness of its fleece. Nowadays, the numerous migrating flocks that graze in the upper valley of the Tigrus and follow the traditional tracks provide a supple wool, very white and with long fibres. In India and Pakistan, countries where carpet production has developed greatly in the last few decades, the indigenous wool is not always of the high quality required for carpet-making. The manufacturers are therefore obliged to import wool from New Zealand and Australia.

A curious "fat-tailed" breed of sheep lives in Iran and Turkestan. When there is copious grazing, the animal's fat is concentrated in the hindquarters and tail, and the growth of wool that develops can weigh up to 44 pounds (20 kilograms). The fat stored there becomes a valuable energy reserve. The wool of sheep from northern Iran is rather coarse and thick, that from Khorassan and Kerman fine and velvety, and that from the Caucasus and Central Asia glossy and very hard-wearing. Goat's hair is also often used (especially for the warp) in rugs from Afghanistan and Turkestan and in those of the Baluchi tribes.

In Persia silk was used formerly only for those rugs destined for the court or for the richest collectors. Today, silk is frequently employed in rugs from Turkey, Iran, India, Kashmir and China. In Iran and Kashmir, silk combined with wool is used fairly often for the pile to give a more lustrous appearance to the carpet. In the Caucasus, silk has never been employed for carpets, but in Turkestan and Afghanistan, it is used to emphasize some motifs in the pattern, while the remaining areas are in wool.

The material chosen for the warp and weft vary with the region: in Turkey (especially in industrialized production), the warp and weft are in cotton, while in some prayer rugs of village origin, they are in wool. In Iran, with the exception of a few regions, cotton is in general use for warp and weft. In the Caucasus, in the past, only wool was employed, while in the modern Caucasian rugs cotton forms both warp and weft.

Wool used for the pile is usually two-ply, that is to say, two strands twisted together. The thickness of the warp and weft threads varies according to the region, but the wool is in multi-ply, from two-ply to sixteen-ply.

Among the nomadic population, shearing time is usually towards the end of spring. Before being clipped, the animal is washed beside a river or lake, or near a well. After shearing, the wool undergoes a second washing in a river or in large basins. Finally, it is thoroughly trodden underfoot and dried in the open air.

Spinning is carried out in a totally primitive fashion. The spinner, holding a bundle of wool under his armpit, begins to twist the yarn, which, as it gradually grows in length, is wound onto a rod. The wool is then ready for the dyeing process. In the factories and in many villages, spinning has become modernized and is carried out partly by machine.

Dyeing

The beauty of the dyes and the harmonious colour combinations are one of the most attractive features of the Oriental rug. The Asian peoples, past masters in the art of dyeing, are skilled not only in obtaining the warm, luminous, restrained tones that enliven their creations, but they can also foresee the chromatic changes to which the rugs will be subjected throughout their life.

Their dyeing method differs from our own in that the Oriental dyer chooses alum as the mordant, rather than bichromate. The entire range of colours can be obtained, from the golden yellow of Kerman to the dark shades of Baluchistan, from the shimmering colours of the flowers of Tabriz to the wonderfully pure tones of Shirvan and Kazak, where varied hues compensate for the geometric austerity of the design. The richness of the chromatic range permits magnificent decorative effects, either through the contrast or the harmony of the colours.

The dyeing formulae, based on plant, animal and mineral substances, have been handed down through the centuries. The most important vegetable colouring is derived from the madder plant, the root of which provides the entire range of pinks and reds. A common plant in Iran, the madder has been familiar in the Near East for a very long time and grows freely almost everywhere, especially in the provinces of Kerman, Zyd and Mazanderan, and in some regions it is cultivated. Imported cochineal is another primary source of red. A reddish yellow is extracted from wild saffron, while cultivated saffron gives a pure yellow, and a light yellow is distilled from the turmeric root. Blue is obtained by soaking and fermenting the blue indigo plant, which grows abundantly in China and India, and was used as long ago as in ancient Egypt. Although indigo and chochineal are not products of Iran, they have been in use for centuries to dye wool for Persian carpets. The rarely used black is an extract of iron oxide and is the only dye of mineral origin.

With these few dyes, shrewdly diluted and skillfully mixed, the Oriental dyer obtains all shades, apart from the natural white of the wool or the browns of camel hair. Sometimes the required amount of dyed wool is not calculated exactly before beginning a rug, especially among the nomadic tribes with their love of the unexpected. Once the wool of one colour is used up, more has to be dyed in order to complete the work, and it is patterns alone. Indeed, each region developed its own designs and jealously maintained its tradition. Each motif had a particular significance, handed down from generation to generation, which revealed the origin of each group of carpets, of which there were an infinite variety.

With a little training, it was fairly easy to differentiate between the six main groups of origin: Asia Minor, Iran, the Caucasus, Afghanistan, India and China. The identification of the exact production centre was, and still is, more difficult and necessitated a preliminary study of styles.

These considerations only hold good for early rugs. Postwar examples are less quiet in tone and different in designs, which are no longer typical of the producing regions. If manufacturers nowadays are also reproducing types of patterns that are foreign to the producing region, the fault—if it can be so termed—lies in the Western taste that has corrupted the design tradition. However, today many of these innovations have come to be considered classics. For some years, the designs of the countries of the Middle East and Turkestan have been commonly reproduced in India and China, so that it is becoming more and more difficult to determine accurately the origin of a rug, unless one is a professional.

The variety of Oriental pattern is infinite, a true reflection of the imagination of the people. The predominance of geometric design might seem the expression of a primitive art, but in reality it represents the product of a remarkably inventive mind. Iconographic limitations have never prevented or hampered the free development of the art which is manifest through the medium of charmingly stylized forms.

Asia Minor can boast of a great variety of styles of patterns: there are charming patterns with broken lines and highly stylized forms that are almost geometric and can sometimes, in consequence, be confused with the motifs of the Caucasus. Ornamentation is often floral with motifs of Persian inspiration. The geometrically patterned Bergamo and Yürük rugs are influenced by the traditional art of the Turkoman tribes of Central Asia, who came to settle in Anatolia at the beginning of the fourteenth century.

In Caucasian rugs a pronounced tendency towards stylization leads to geometric designs and scattered human, animal and floral motifs on a dense ground of small lozenges, pointed stars, squares, triangles and other motifs, arranged without symmetry. There are a few rugs with rather large patterns and broad lines, which are exceptions.

The products of Central Asia and Turkestan, which also adopted geometric patterns, show a marked predilection for symmetry and regularity, both in form and in composition.

The ancient "running dog" frieze animates the borders of Caucasian rugs even today, especially those knotted by the carpet-makers of Soumak.

One motif peculiar to Turkoman rugs, especially those from Bukhara, is the so-called "flight of eagles" motif, an heraldic symbol found in the lozenge shapes, in white on a rust ground, arranged diagonally in two opposite corners. On observation these shapes reveal the eagle with outspread wings which inspired them. The Turkoman tribes and the ancient tribes of Asia Minor have a great affection for the "Salor rose, or *gul*" motif, greatly cherished by the tribe of the same name,

Symbols Found on Chinese Rugs

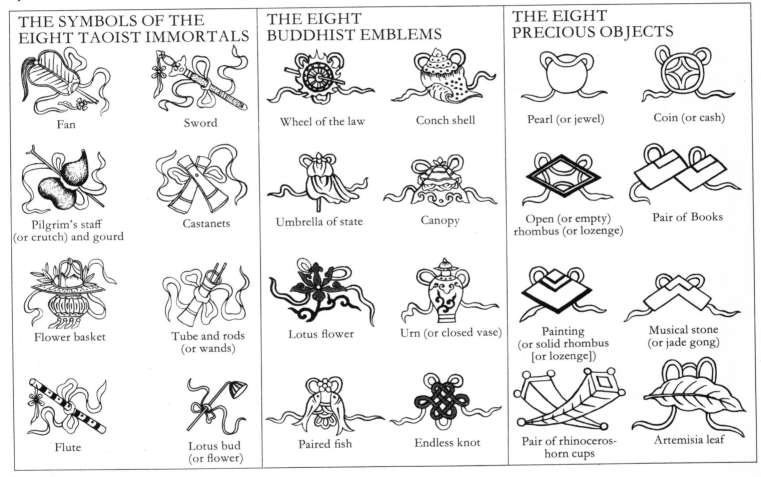

THE SYMBOLS OF THE EIGHT TAOIST IMMORTALS		THE EIGHT BUDDHIST EMBLEMS		THE EIGHT PRECIOUS OBJECTS	
Fan	Sword	Wheel of the law	Conch shell	Pearl (or jewel)	Coin (or cash)
Pilgrim's staff (or crutch) and gourd	Castanets	Umbrella of state	Canopy	Open (or empty) rhombus (or lozenge)	Pair of Books
Flower basket	Tube and rods (or wands)	Lotus flower	Urn (or closed vase)	Painting (or solid rhombus [or lozenge])	Musical stone (or jade gong)
Flute	Lotus bud (or flower)	Paired fish	Endless knot	Pair of rhinoceros-horn cups	Artemisia leaf

loom generally permits the production of more evenly woven rugs. In Kerman, this type of loom usually has metal rollers. In China, looms have been improved by the use of tension screws in the crossbeams. Generally speaking, roller-beam looms are being used more and more throughout the rug-producing countries.

Every loom, whether vertical or horizontal, possesses a very simple mechanism that permits the knotter to separate the warp into two sheets, so that they can be reversed after each shoot of the weft, or horizontal threads. In the single-weft process of weaving, the warp threads all lie in the same plane, while with a double weft, the warp threads are pulled forward alternately, so that those forming the back of the carpet remain unseen on the front of the finished product. The latter method has the advantage of providing a more compact foundation for the carpet.

To manufacture a rug, the weaver begins by making a selvedge: several shoots of weft are passed to make a narrow band, like a rough cloth, intended to provide a firm edge for the knotting. There are different sorts of knots, the most common being the Turkish knot and the Persian knot, also called the Ghiordes knot and the Senneh knot respectively.

The Turkish or Ghiordes Knot

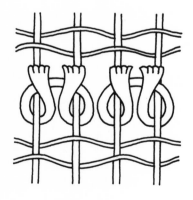

As knotting begins, three or four lateral warp threads are left free; with the to-and-fro movement of the weft, they will form a very narrow but vital selvedge down the sides of the rug.

The Ghiordes knot is tied around two adjacent warp threads, each of which are encircled by the strand of

wool; the ends of the woolen strand reappear between these two warp threads. The process is then repeated. A loop of wool about 2 or 3 centimetres (0.8 or 1.2 in.) in length is left between each knot until the last warp thread of the row. With the aid of two shed-sticks to separate the warp threads, two shoots of weft are then passed, forwards and backwards, across the whole breadth of the carpet, including the lateral threads that bear no knots. After each shoot, the weft is compressed against the row of knots with a heavy metal comb. Finally, a new row of knots is begun following the same procedure, which is repeated until completion of the knotting. Then the loops of wool are cut to form tufts which, after clipping, constitute the pile of the carpet.

The Persian or Senneh Knot

This knot is also tied onto two adjacent warp threads, after the first few have been set aside at the side for the selvedge. But, unlike the Turkish knot, in the Persian knot only one of the warp threads is encircled by the strand of wool, which merely passes behind the other warp thread, so that the ends of the woolen strand appear separately: the first between the original two warp threads, and the second between the two subsequent ones. Each Senneh knot is separated from its neighbour by a loop, which is cut after the passage of the weft. The Persian knot can be tied equally well from right to left or viceversa, which is why it is sometimes called the "two-handed" knot. When several knotters are working on the same carpet and using Persian knots, one begins his knotting from the right and one from the left.

Knots can also be tied on three warp threads, by holding two threads together while keeping one separate, or on four threads if these are divided into two pairs. This procedure is becoming increasingly widespread in the Far East, for the knotting progresses more rapidly, to the detriment, however, of the hard-wearing qualities of the carpet.

The Tibetan Knot

The Tibetan method of tying knots is different from that used by all other carpet-makers of the world. It is sometimes termed Senneh looping. The Tibetans employ a round metal rod, around which they pass the woolen yarn for the pile; however, they do not cut the wool after tying each knot (the usual practice). They wait until they have reached the end of a row of knots of the same colour. With this method of knotting progress is good and wool is not wasted. The resulting carpet

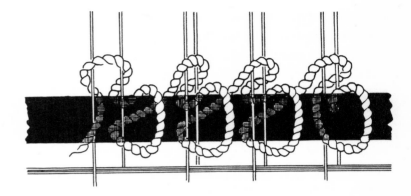

is knotted quite tightly but not finely, because Tibetans use very thick wool (of up to eight strands of yarn) which is doubled when the knots are tied on the rod. In the Tibetan knot one knot is tied on each pair of warp threads—as in the Turkish knot—but the arrangement of the strands is different.

Choosing and Caring for Oriental Carpets

Oriental carpets generally blend easily into the interior of Western homes: the colours are peaceful and harmonious and, as a result, do not detract from the beauty of wall coverings or other furnishings.

It is usually advisable to choose a compact rug of good wool. Some Oriental rugs have a slacker texture than others, and the use to which the rug will be put (wall hanging, runner in an entry, area rug, etc.) should be considered before a choice is made. A carpet must always be examined on the reverse, where the pattern of the front appears again more or less distinctly. For most uses, the finer, more compact and careful the knotting, the better the carpet.

An Oriental carpet should last a long time—for several generations—according to the use made of it. Rugs hung on walls can last for centuries as the magnificent examples in the world's museums prove.

The precautions for properly conserving a rug are very simple: dust and moths are the insidious enemies. Oriental carpets need only be beaten very rarely; vacuum cleaners ensure sufficient cleaning, and the warp and weft threads of a carpet that has been hung over a rail suffer from beating. Ideally an Oriental rug should be spread on the grass or fresh snow for beating on the reverse; this not only cleans the carpet but also helps to restore the colours. (Allow a carpet to cool before spreading it on snow or it will become wet.) Antique rugs as well as those made of silk need special care: they should not be beaten and should be vacuumed only lightly.

During the summer, if a house is vacant for any length of time, there is the risk that moths will attack the carpets. Use commercial insecticides to prevent this.

If the carpet suffers the smallest tear, or the pile is worn away to expose warp and weft threads, a specialist should be consulted to remake the missing knots. With carpets of recent manufacture, weft threads adjacent to the fringe often come loose, leaving a row of knots unbound. These, in turn, become undone little by little and may eventually destroy the entire carpet. The danger can be overcome by the prompt intervention of a carpet restorer.

Pl. 1   Shirvan / Chirvan

Pl. 2   Shirvan / Chirvan

Pl. 3   Shirvan / Chirvan

Pl. 4   Shirvan / Chirvan

Pl. 5   Shirvan Akstava / Chirvan Akstafa

Pl. 6   Kuba / Kouba

Pl. 7   Kuba / Kouba

Pl. 8   Perepedil / Pérépédil

Pl. 9   Daghestan

Pl. 10   Daghestan

Pl. 11   Gendje / Gandja

Pl. 12   Kazak Lori-Pambak / Kazak Lori Pambak

Pl. 13   Kazak Fachralo

Pl. 14   Kazak

Pl. 15   Kazak

Pl. 16   Karabagh / Karabakh

Pl. 17   Soumak

Pl. 18   Yahyali

Pl. 19   Konya / Konia

Pl. 20   Milas

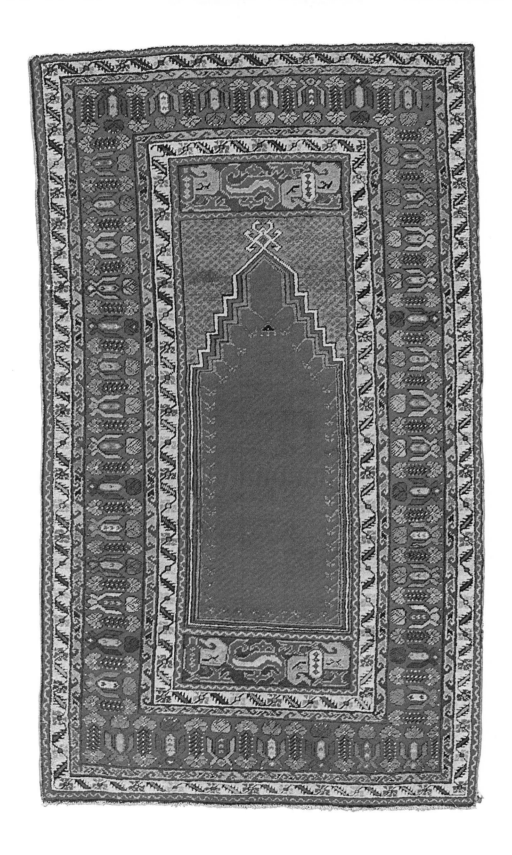

Pl. 21   Kirsehir / Kırséhir

Pl. 22   Cal

Pl. 23   Sivas

Pl. 24   Hereke / Héréké

Pl. 25   Shiraz / Chiraz

Pl. 26   Kerman-Afshar / Afchar

Pl. 27   Kerman / Kirman

Pl. 28   Kalar Dashti / Kelardasht

Pl. 29   Karaja / Karadja

Pl. 30   Mir

Pl. 31   Sarouk

Pl. 32 Yalameh / Yalamé

Pl. 33   Isfahan / Ispahan

Pl. 34   Qum / Qom

Pl. 35   Kashgai / Kachgai

Pl. 36   Kashan / Kachan

Pl. 37   Bijar / Bidjar

Pl. 38   Koliayeh

Pl. 39   Ardebil / Ardébil

Pl. 40   Sarab

Pl. 41   Mishkin / Mechkin

Pl. 42   Birjand / Birdjand

Pl. 43   Varamin

Pl. 44   Tafresh

Pl. 45   Nain / Naïn

Pl. 46   Heriz / Hériz

Pl. 47   Luristan / Louristan

Pl. 48   Baluchi / Béloudj

Pl. 49   Mashhad / Machad

Pl. 50   Maslaghan / Mazlaghan

Pl. 51   Semnan

Pl. 52   Injilas

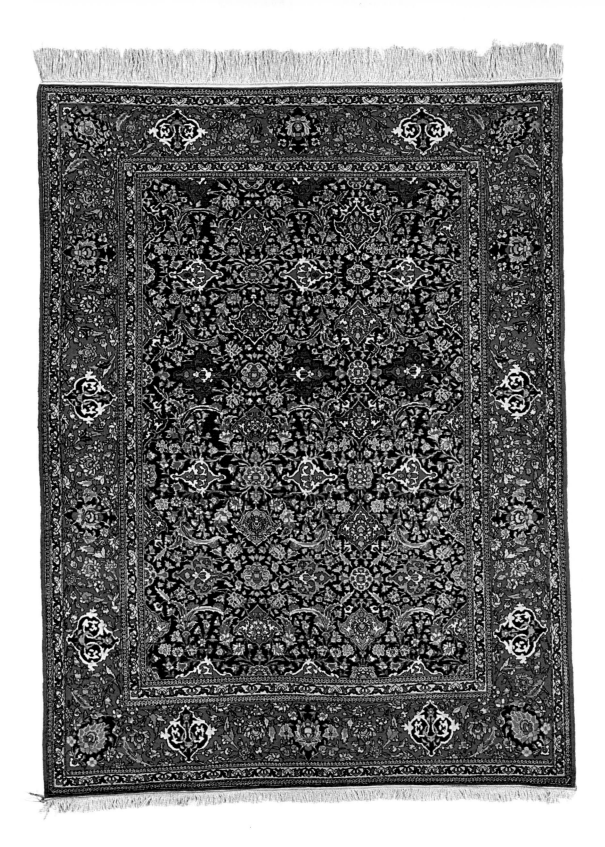

Pl. 53   Isfahan / Ispahan

Pl. 54   Joshagan / Jowshaqan

Pl. 55   Tabriz

Pl. 56   Tabriz (Hajji Jalil) / Tabriz

Pl. 57   Feraghan / Férahan

Pl. 58   Mahal

Pl. 59   Kashan / Kachan

Pl. 60   Bakhtiari / Bakhtiar

Pl. 61   Senneh

Pl. 62   Yazd

Pl. 63   Turkoman / Turcoman

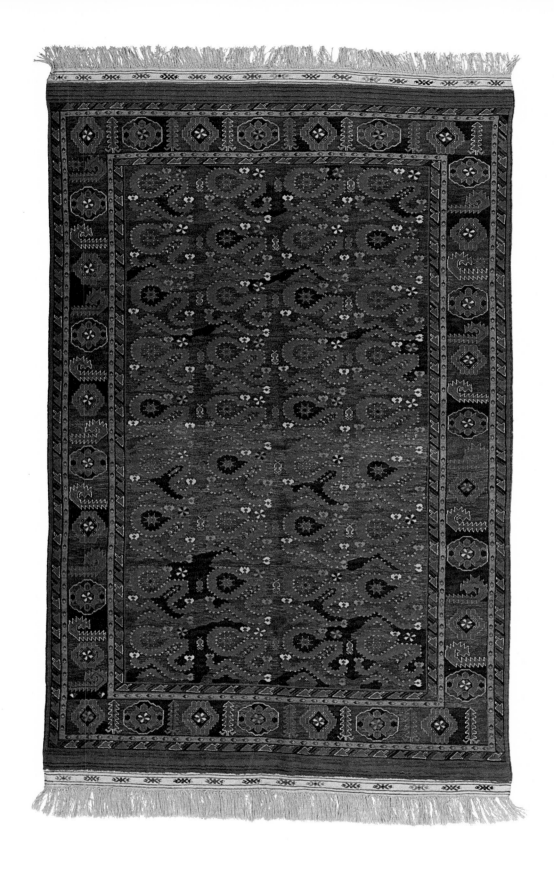

Pl. 64   Beshir / Béchir

Pl. 65   Bukhara / Boukhara

Pl. 66 Yomud / Yomoud

Pl. 67   Yomud Engsi / Yomoud Ensi

Pl. 68   Afghan

Pl. 69   Ersari-Afghan

Pl. 70   Kashmir / Cachemire

Pl. 71   Kashmir / Cachemire

Pl. 72   Kashmir / Cachemire

Pl. 73   Bhadohi

Pl. 74   Bhadohi

Pl. 75　Ningxia

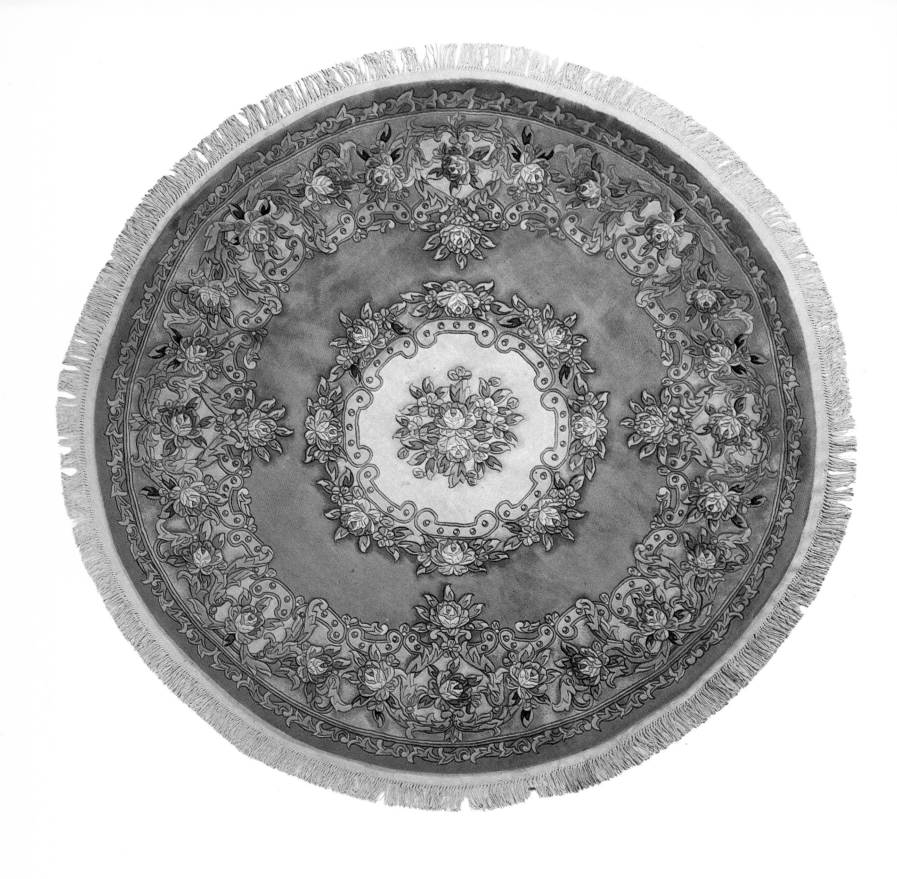

Pl. 76 Shanghai

Pl. 77   Ürümqi / Urumqi

Pl. 78   Xizang (Tibet) / Tibet

Pl. 79   Beijing

Pl. 80 Baotou

THE CAUCASUS

Pl. 1 SHIRVAN

(USSR) dated 1923
Dimensions: 69 × 53 inches (175 × 135 cm)
Turkish knot: 201 knots per sq. inch (312,800 per sq. metre)
   11.5 knots per inch width (46 per 10 cm width)
   17.5 knots per inch length (68 per 10 cm length)
Warp: four strands of natural wool
Weft: two strands of natural wool
Pile: two strands of wool
12 colours: 2 blues, 1 ochre, 1 white, 1 black, 3 reds, 1 orange, 1 grey, 1 yellow, 1 pink

This rug bears the date of its manufacture—the year 1341 of the Hegira, corresponding to 1923.

The field with a royal blue ground is entirely covered with flowers and other motifs, including small crosses, rams' horns and birds. It is surrounded by seven borders; the main one, with a brownish beige ground, has a decoration of pairs of double keys which enclose a rosette. Each key contains a small "S". On both sides of the main border, and separated from it by two narrow bands with a red ground, there are two bands with white grounds, each decorated with stars surrounded by squares, alternating with diagonal bars. Two more narrow bands, this time with blue grounds, run round the outside of the rug.

The soft yet warm colours of this rug blend well together, giving it a remarkably harmonious appearance which shows the highly developed artistic sense of its designer.

Pl. 2 SHIRVAN

(USSR) *circa* 1910
Dimensions: 117 × 60 inches (297 × 152 cm)
Turkish knot: 113 knots per sq. inch (176,400 per sq. metre)
   9 knots per inch width (36 per 10 cm width)
   12.5 knots per inch length (49 per 10 cm length)
Warp: three stands of natural wool
Single weft: two strands of natural wool
Pile: two strands of wool
12 colours: 1 red, 3 blues, 2 greens, 1 orange, 1 yellow, 1 white, 1 black, 1 gold, 1 brown

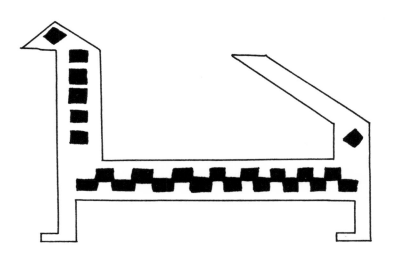

Pl. 3 SHIRVAN

(USSR) early 20th century
Dimensions: 60 × 40 inches (152 × 102 cm)
Turkish knot: 128 knots per sq. inch (197,600 per sq. metre)
   10 knots per inch width (38 per 10 cm width)
   13 knots per inch length (52 per 10 cm length)
Warp: three strands of natural beige wool
Double weft: three strands of grey wool
Pile: two strands of wool
12 colours: 3 reds, 3 blues, 2 greens, 1 white, 1 brownish black, 1 gold, 1 yellow

One is immediately struck by the rich colours of this rug, which are enhanced by the great variety of motifs covering its field. One notices, first of all, the row of six hexagons decorated with flowers and latch-hooks on a dark blue ground; the field on each side of this row is scattered with a multitude of various animals with two, three or four legs, numerous flowers, rosettes and *boteh-miri* motifs, some with a central cross. At each end of the row of hexagons, one finds a very elongated motif with a zigzag outline, a central decoration of leaves and a small rosette surmounted by three crosses on a gold ground.

The decoration of the main border, also with a gold ground, belongs to the wine-glass type of motif and also contains oak leaves; it is flanked by two floral bands on red grounds. The field is framed by a red zigzag band, followed by a narrow band with white snakes on a brown ground.

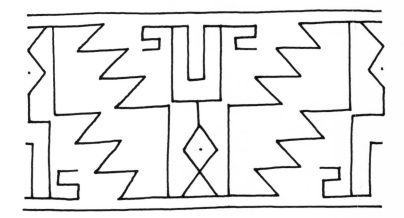

The decoration of this piece, which dates from the beginning of the century, is interesting. A large rectangular motif terminates at either end in an octagon. This encloses two smaller octagons, flanked by two small rectangles, which are in turn placed on either side of a central octagon that is of the same colour as the field. Note the four additional triangles at the corners of the

Pl. 4 SHIRVAN

(USSR) late 19th century
Dimensions: 114 × 45.5 inches (290 × 115 cm)
Turkish knot: 130 knots per sq. inch (201,600 per sq. metre)
    9 knots per inch width (36 per 10 cm width)
    14.5 knots per inch length (56 per 10 cm length)
Warp: three strands, each consisting of a mixture of natural brown and white woolen threads tightly twisted together
Weft: three strands of fine, white wool
Pile: two strands of wool
10 colours: 1 red, 2 blues, 1 gold, 2 beige, 1 green, 1 black, 1 white, 1 violet

octagons. Thus there is a very well balanced arrangement of geometric motifs. Another point worth mentioning is the remarkable use of double latch-hooks as a decorative element in all details of the central motif, whether in the terminal octagons, in the white crosses that decorate the central octagon or in the four small motifs surrounding each cross, separated by a double rectangle trimmed with a flower.

The principal border is of the wine-glass type and is enclosed on both sides by a zigzag band, and at the outer edge by a band of small multicoloured lozenges. The harmony of the composition corresponds with that of the colours.

Five medallions are arranged on a blue ground scattered with flowers; two of these medallions have a red ground, and three a white one. Each medallion is decorated with a central lozenge and two pairs of large latch-hooks; enclosing them is a gold band containing motifs representing a sort of comb. On either side of the field, between the medallions, are four rectangles, each enclosing a large triangular motif that has a latch-hook coming from one of its points and a design resembling the teeth of a comb along the longest side. The other motifs in the field are essentially floral. The main border has a design of leaves alternating with the so-called wine-glass motif on a white ground. It is flanked by two floral borders.

This extremely fine Shirvan with its very warm, glowing colours is in a good state of preservation.

Pl. 5 SHIRVAN AKSTAVA

(USSR) *circa* 1870
Dimensions: 117.5 × 45 inches (298 × 114 cm)
Turkish knot: 81 knots per sq. inch (122,500 per sq. metre)
    9 knots per inch width (35 per 10 cm width)
    9 knots per inch length (35 per 10 cm length)
Warp: two strands of natural beige wool
Weft: three strands of unbleached cotton
Pile: two strands of wool
10 colours: 2 reds, 3 blues, 2 greens, 1 brown, 1 black, 1 gold

The field with a dark blue ground contains four star-shaped polygons, two of which are red, one white and one blue. These polygons have a decoration of *boteh*, stylized flowers and latch-hooks. Between the polygons

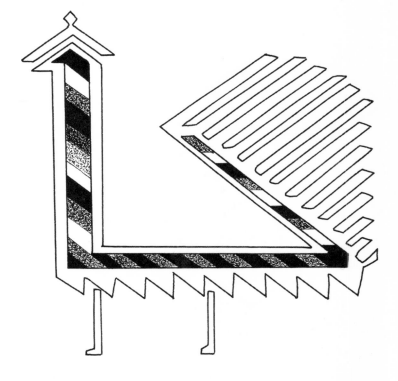

are five pairs of stylized birds, looking rather like peacocks fanning their tail feathers. All except one pair face in the same direction. The remainder of the field is filled with *boteh*, rosettes, flowers and small animals, the latter being frequently used in Shirvan rugs of this type.

The main border, with a white ground, contains a great variety of squares and rectangles decorated with different motifs (*boteh*, rosettes, latch-hooks and flowers). It is surrounded by two borders, each having the same snake design (of Persian origin), one on a blue ground, the other on a green ground.

This rug is characterized by its beautiful, warm and bright colours and by its soft pile.

Pl. 6 KUBA

(USSR) *circa* 1920
Dimensions: 79.5 × 45.5 inches (202 × 116 cm)
Turkish knot: 85 knots per sq. inch (134,400 per sq. metre)
    8 knots per inch width (32 per 10 cm width)
    10.5 knots per inch length (42 per 10 cm length)
Warp: three strands of natural beige and brown wool finishing in multiple knots
Weft: two strands of natural beige and brown wool
Pile: two strands of wool
10 colours: 2 reds, 1 blue, 1 reddish brown, 1 beige, 1 grey, 1 green, 1 gold, 1 brownish black, 1 white

Most of the field with a light blue ground is filled by a red motif outlined by a band with a white ground. Inside

this red motif is a row of five octagons decorated with latch-hooks and flowers. The decoration of the field is completed by animals, flowers, a scattering of "S" motifs and a line of red latch-hooks, which forms an outline to the whole design.

The border consists of a number of narrow bands: first of all, nearest the field, is a red and black Georgian border flanked by two bands of stars; these are followed by three floral bands, two of which (on black grounds) frame the third, which has a design of carnations on a red ground.

The vividness of the colours and the boldness of the geometrical composition, combined with the beautiful sheen of the wool, are all factors which contribute to the appeal of this rug.

Pl. 7 KUBA

(USSR) *circa* 1870
Dimensions: 73 × 50 inches (185 × 128 cm)
Turkish knot: 117 knots per sq. inch (182,000 per sq. metre)
    9 knots per inch width (35 per 10 cm width)
    13 knots per inch length (52 per 10 cm length)
Warp: two strands of natural beige wool
Weft: two strands of natural beige wool
Pile: two strands of wool
7 colours: 2 reds, 2 blues, 1 green, 1 black, 1 white

The most striking feature of this rug is the finishing of its borders in a manner typical of carpets from the Caucasian region of Kuba: at each end is a band, several

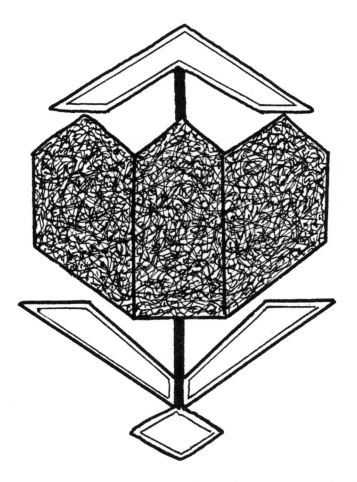

Although this rug has no main border, its framing is nevertheless impressive: the field is surrounded by eleven bands, the two widest pairs being less than two inches wide. These bands, which have a design of stylized flowers, are separated by red and white striped lines.

For its age, this Kuba is in a remarkably good state of preservation.

Pl. 8 PEREPEDIL

(USSR, the region to the north of Kuba) end of 19th century
Dimensions: 81.5 × 56 inches (207 × 142 cm)
Turkish knot: 182 knots per sq. inch (285,600 per sq. metre)
  13 knots per inch width (51 per 10 cm width)
  14 knots per inch length (56 per 10 cm length)
Warp: four strands of natural beige wool finishing in multiple knots at each end
Weft: four strands of unbleached cotton
Pile: two strands of wool
10 colours: 2 reds, 2 blues, 1 green, 1 greyish brown, 1 gold, 1 white, 1 black, 1 brownish beige

inches wide, of Soumak stitch in blue cotton; on both sides the rug has a narrow border of blue cotton. The warp threads have been tied together to form a fringe of knots at each side.

The decoration of this rug is restrained: the red field is covered with lozenges with notched outlines; these lozenges contain trees and stylized flowers in alternate rows, and at one side of the field there are two different motifs of a small human figure and a comb.

The dark blue field is occupied by seven *wurma* (ram's head motifs), all but one pointing in the same direction; no two are alike either in design or in colour. They are separated from each other by large stylized flowers and by animals with four or six legs, some of which have a comblike crest. A row of six *wurma*, different in design from the ones in the centre, runs the length of the two longest sides of the field. They alternate with a narrow

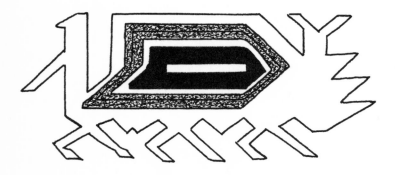

band of of flowers containing a small cross in its centre; this cross has given rise to the hypothesis that the weaver was an Armenian.

The main border with a red ground contains the *kufi* motif that was used as a decoration in the carpets which Holbein painted in his pictures. There are three bands on each side of the main border. Two of these are repeated twice on either side of this main border; one has carnations on a brownish black ground; the other, stars on a white ground.

This rug is an admirable piece, of outstanding refinement and harmonious colours.

Pl. 9 DAGHESTAN

(USSR) late 19th century
Dimensions: 59.5 × 46.5 inches (151 × 118 cm)
Turkish knot: 98 knots per sq. inch (153,000 per sq. metre)
   8.5 knots per inch width (34 per 10 cm width)
   11.5 knots per inch length (45 per 10 cm length)
Warp: two strands of natural brown wool and one strand of natural beige wool

Weft: one strand of white wool and two strands of white cotton
Pile: two strands of wool
10 colours: 2 reds, 3 blues, 1 reddish brown, 1 green, 1 gold, 1 brownish black, 1 white

The ivory ground of the field throws into sharp relief this prayer rug's *mihrab*, outlined by a blue band decorated with sloping bars. The general decoration of the field consists of stylized birds arranged evenly in rows. At the apex of the niche is a small red polygon containing a white rectangle which, in turn, contains a tiny black square. A row of bluish black saw-teeth runs round the field.

The framing consists of five borders, separated by six narrow bands. The main border, with a red ground, has a design of the "stepped" type in various colours. On each side, it is framed by a border with a brownish black ground, in which crosses alternate with "X" shapes. These borders are highlighted by narrow bands with a design of black and white dots.

The charm of this rug lies in the great variety of its motifs and the soft colours used.

Pl. 10 DAGHESTAN

(USSR) late 19th century
Dimensions: 94.5 × 50.5 inches (240 × 128 cm)
Turkish knot: 90 knots per sq. inch (140,000 per sq. metre)
  10 knots per inch width (39 per 10 cm width)
  9 knots per inch length (36 per 10 cm length)
Warp: three strands of natural beige and brown wool, consisting of two beige strands and one brown strand twisted together
Weft: three strands of natural white wool
Pile: two strands of wool
10 colours: 1 red, 2 blues, 1 green, 1 light brown, 1 beige, 1 straw yellow, 1 gold, 1 dark brown, 1 white

The field is filled by three rectangular medallions, linked together and forming, at either end of the rug, a vase-shaped motif. Each rectangle has a similar decoration: stars, stylized spiders, flowers, "S" shapes and small squares divided into four and each containing a central lozenge with a dentate outline, which itself contains a tiny rectangle. Several examples of the same motif are also found outside the medallions, where they are scattered at random on the red ground of the field, along with other small motifs such as a five-legged dog and a farmyard animal. The random positioning of all these small irregular motifs makes them all the more appealing.

The same lack of regularity is a feature of the outermost border where the weaver has used, on a dark brown ground, not only the classical carnation, but also round flowers of various shapes and colours. The white main border has a "crab" design, and the inner border repeats the carnation motif of the outer one.

The colours of this rug are warm and harmonious, its wool is lustrous and its overall appearance is very attractive.

Pl. 11 GENDJE

(USSR, Kirowbad region, formerly Gendje)
circa 1920
Dimensions: 129 × 56 inches (327 × 145 cm)
Turkish knot: 42 knots per sq. inch (64,400 per sq. metre)
  6 knots per inch width (23 per 10 cm width)
  7 knots per inch length (28 per 10 cm length)
Warp: three strands of natural beige/brown wool
Double weft: two strands of red wool
Pile: two strands of wool of medium thickness, with natural sheen
8 colours: 2 reds, 3 blues, 1 gold, 1 white, 1 brownish black

This rug is a classical example of early manufacture, which, alas, has disappeared gradually from the market. There are numerous irregularities in design which give it its charm and for which one can search in vain in present-day carpets. The same type of design can still be found, but the treatment is strict and exact, and the borders are simplified.

In this piece, the four octagons of the medallions are decorated with motifs like stylized serpents, called

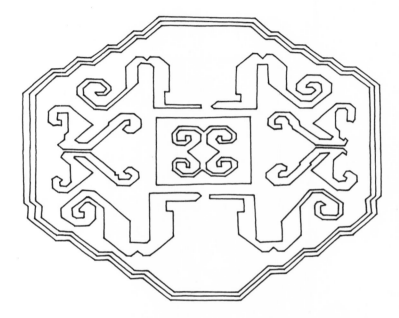

Wolkenband in Germany. The main border, of the double latch-hook type, is surrounded by two narrow bands strewn with stars. The field has an irregular decoration of stars, double latch-hooks and stylized flowers. The very soft, warm colouring adds to the charm of this example.

Pl. 12 KAZAK LORI-PAMBAK

(USSR) *circa* 1920
Dimensions: 110 × 71.5 inches (280 × 182 cm)
Turkish knot: 42 knots per sq. inch (64,800 per sq. metre)
  6 knots per inch width (24 per 10 cm width)
  7 knots per inch length (27 per 10 cm length)
Warp: two strands of natural wool in a mixture of beige

and white, looped at one end and with multiple knots at the other
Weft: two strands of red wool
Pile: two strands of wool
8 colours: 2 reds, 2 blues, 1 green, 1 yellow, 1 brownish black, 1 white

Standing on a red ground, a large white octagonal medallion is framed on either side by a smaller medallion of the same shape as the large one and with the same red ground. The decoration of the field is completed by a

sparse scattering of motifs—lozenges, crosses, rectangles and an inscription which mentions the name of the weaver (Rahim Karim Oghli).

The field is framed by eight narrow bands and a border. The latter is decorated with the "hands of Fatima" (?) motif and large red stars on a white ground.

All the motifs in this rug are distinguished by their large, simple and very geometrical shapes—a typical feature of Lori-Pambak designs. The colours are warm and bright, and the pile has an attractive sheen.

Pl. 13   KAZAK FACHRALO

(USSR) dated 1913
Dimensions: 76.5 × 55 inches (194 × 140 cm)
Turkish knot: 72 knots per sq. inch (112,000 per sq. metre)
   8 knots per inch width (32 per 10 cm width)
   9 knots per inch length (35 per 10 cm length)
Warp: three strands of natural beige wool
Weft: two strands of red wool
Pile: two strands of wool
7 colours: 2 reds, 1 midnight blue, 1 turquoise, 1 straw yellow, 1 brown, 1 white

This Kazak prayer rug has a *mihrab* of modest dimensions in which its date of manufacture, 1331 of the Hegira (1913), is inscribed in a small cartouche. The centre of the field has a red ground and is filled by two large crosses, each containing one or two stars of Solomon, so called because, according to legend, this king wore on his finger an eight-pointed diamond, the "star of the

Medes". The decoration of the field is completed by four small octagons of a deeper red, each bearing a stylized scorpion, and by small flowers, latch-hooks, two motifs ornamented with stylized glasses, animals and "S" shapes.

A blue band with flowers frames the field and the *mihrab*, and, at the end farthest from the *mihrab*, runs round three sides of a square with a blue ground, in the centre of which lies a beautiful, straw-coloured rosette. The first border surrounding the field is decorated with flowers having a multicoloured line trailing between

them; this is wavy along the length of the rug and angular across the width. Next comes the main border with a white ground, in which trees alternate with fairly wide, branched rods decorated with "S" shapes. Round the outside of the rug runs a turquoise border bearing multi-coloured diagonal strips.

As always with Fachralo carpets, the pile is very soft and fairly short.

Pl. 14 KAZAK

(USSR) *circa* 1900
Dimensions: 71 × 48 inches (180 × 122 cm)
Turkish knot: 49 knots per sq. inch (75,400 per sq. metre)
  6.5 knots per inch width (26 per 10 cm width)
  7.5 knots per inch length (29 per 10 cm length)
Warp: two strands of natural wool
Weft: two strands of red wool
Pile: two strands of wool
7 colours: 1 red, 1 blue, 1 white, 1 green, 1 violet, 1 gold, 1 black

On a field with a red ground, this prayer rug has a *mihrab* with a white ground, decorated mainly with latch-hooks; these latch-hooks are found again inside the rectangle with its gold ground which is contained within the central medallion. There are forty identical latch-hooks in all, not counting the pair that stand on either side of the arch of the *mihrab*. The main border, decorated with zigzags, has a gold ground.

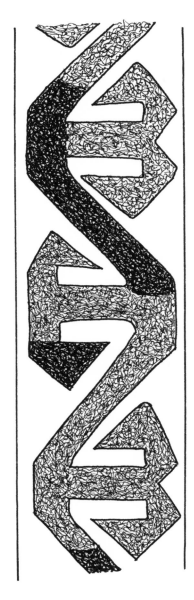

Pl. 15 KAZAK

(USSR) late 19th century
Dimensions: 94 × 62.5 inches (238 × 159 cm)
Turkish knot: 65 knots per sq. inch (96,600 per sq. metre)
  6 knots per inch width (23 per 10 cm width)
  10.5 knots per inch length (42 per 10 cm length)
Warp: three strands of natural white wool
Weft: two strands of red wool
Pile: two strands of thick wool
7 colours: 1 red, 2 blues, 1 green, 1 white, 1 brownish black, 1 yellow

The very simple ornamentation and the fairly thick pile of this rug lead one to believe that its comes from a Caucasian village. Its colours are warm and harmonious.

Two distinguishing features of Kazak carpets made in the mountain villages of the Caucasus are a rather coarse wool and a thick pile. To these might be added another feature—a design which is usually very simple and composed of rather large motifs.

The field of this rug is filled by four medallions; although their shape is similar to that of the *guls* of Turkestan, the latch-hooks surrounding them and also appearing inside the medallions are typically Caucasian. The predominant colour of the field is a very warm red. The colour green is used in the medallions—a quite unusual occurrence. At one end of the field is a row of motifs with double latch-hooks, but this is not repeated at the other end.

In the main border, which is of considerable width, the latch-hooks can again be seen, this time surrounding triangular motifs, on a white ground.

Pl. 16 KARABAGH

(USSR) *circa* 1920
Dimensions: 124 × 53 inches (315 × 134 cm)
Turkish knot: 61 knots per sq. inch (95,200 per sq. metre)
   9 knots per inch width (34 per 10 cm width)
   7 knots per inch length (28 per 10 cm length)
Warp: three strands of wool
Double weft: beige wool
Pile: two strands of wool
12 colours: 3 reds, 3 blues, 2 browns, 1 white, 1 brownish black, 1 orange, 1 beige

Four bright red medallions of jagged form, decorated with large flowers, occupy most of the field. A series of symmetrically arranged motifs fills up the remainder.

Apart from stylized flowers, one can particularly distinguish some four-legged animals that look more like cocks than dogs. The principal border of double latch-hooks is surrounded by two bands called "serpent borders".

This example is of early manufacture, but the colours have remained strong.

Pl. 17   SOUMAK

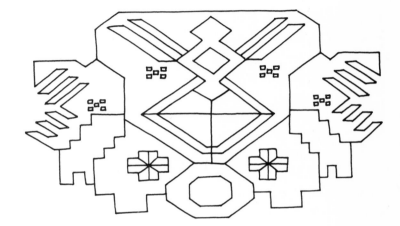

(USSR) *circa* 1930
Dimensions: 103 × 68 inches (262 × 172 cm)
Weaving in Soumak technique carried out in wool
Warp: two strands of natural beige and brown wool
Double weft: one of natural grey wool, the other of red wool, partly brown
10 colours: 3 reds, 2 browns, 2 blues, 1 white,
1 brownish black, 1 green

The Soumak rug differs in technique from knotted pile rugs; it is woven flat, with the wool forming the right side of the rug uncut when it passes onto the reverse side, which gives the latter a rather irregular appearance. Soumak rugs have been produced for a long time in the region of Ortostal (Daghestan) and in the village of Kusary in Azerbaijan.

The field of this rug is covered with fifteen similar geometric medallions; in each there are two octagons and two lozenges, then four motifs in the form of double combs and another decorated with a rose in its centre.

The principal border is narrower at the two ends than at the sides and the design of the ends also differs from the sides: at the sides, the border is filled with interlaced "Y" shapes, while elsewhere it is trimmed with large latch-hooks.

The charm of the Soumak rug lies in its colouring, as is the case with all Caucasian rugs.

TURKEY

Pl. 18 YAHYALI

(Kayseri region) 1970
Dimensions: 78 × 46 inches (197 × 117 cm)
Turkish knot: 100 knots per sq. inch (155,800 per sq. metre)
   9.5 knots per inch width (38 per 10 cm width)
   10 knots per inch length (41 per 10 cm length)

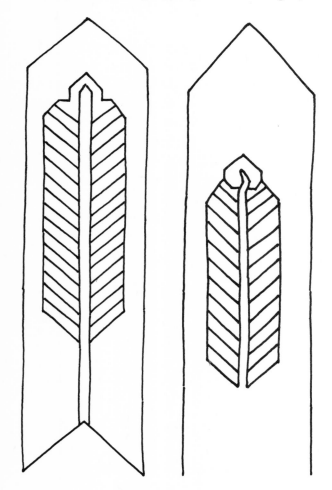

Warp: two strands of wool
Double weft: of red and brown wool
Pile: two strands of wool of medium thickness, chemically washed
12 colours: 3 reds, 2 blues, 2 greens, 2 yellows, 1 white, 1 brownish black, 1 grey

This is a prayer rug of particular type, in which the *mihrab* fills only part of the field. Among other motifs are a mosque flanked by two slender columns terminating in a hand; exactly above is a lamp intended to give light to the believer. Around the *mihrab* are elongated motifs, each decorated with a stylized tree, and high up, two small pendentives bearing an inscription. The two "flower beds" above and below the *mihrab* are decorated with large flowers (daisies?).

A small grey band trimmed with leaves runs all round the field and the flower beds. Another floral band precedes the principal border of rosettes alternating with double latch-hooks. Lastly, the outer band is decorated with the old Persian *medahil* motif.

Pl. 19 KONYA

1970
Dimensions: 70 × 43 inches (179 × 110 cm)
Turkish knot: 69 knots per sq. inch (106,400 per sq. metre)
   7 knots per inch width (28 per 10 cm width)
   9.5 knots per inch length (38 per 10 cm length)
Warp: two strands of wool
Single weft: two strands of red wool

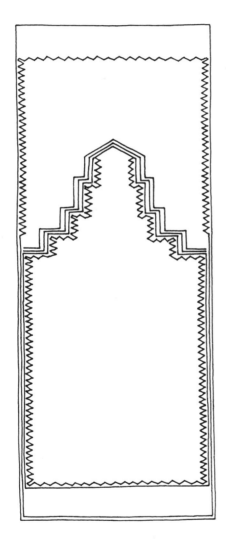

Pile: two strands of wool of medium thickness
8 colours: 1 red, 1 blue, 1 mauve, 1 green, 1 yellow,
1 white, 1 brownish black, 1 beige

Konya, a town in Anatolia of about 125,000 inhabitants,
is also the chief town of the province of the same name.

It is situated at an altitude of 3,366 feet on the edge of a vast plain which occupies the centre of the Anatolian plateau. Its origins go back to the third millennium B.C. Towards the eleventh century, Konya became the capital of the Seljukid sultanate of Roum. It remains one of the principal towns of present-day Turkey.

In the twelfth century, rugs from Konya were already held in high repute, since Marco Polo declares that he had seen the most beautiful carpets in the world in this town.

The example shown here is a prayer rug. The main border, of Georgian (Caucasus) type, is surrounded by two bands decorated with classical *shekeri* motifs (broken lines and rosettes) of Iranian origin. On the two narrow bands that complete the border, the same variation of the double "T" border is repeated: on a yellow ground for the outer strip, and on a white ground for the inner one. The major part of the field is occupied by the *mihrab* with a strong red ground, devoid of decorative details, the outline of which is emphasized by a yellow notched band. The triangular top of the *mihrab*, cut out in steps, is crowned by a tree of life flanked by two large motifs which vaguely recall the carnations of the eighteenth century. At the foot and above the prayer arch, two flower beds of rather smaller scale and very simple style repeat the motif of the steps. A two-coloured kilim weave frames the rug at both ends.

Pl. 20 MILAS

1960
Dimensions: 71 × 49 inches (181 × 125 cm)

Warp: two strands of light natural wool
Double weft: of brown wool
Pile: two strands of wool of medium thickness
8 colours: 2 reds, 1 blue, 1 yellow, 1 green, 1 white,
1 brownish black, 1 brown

Milas, a small town of approximately 12,000 inhabitants, is situated quite close to the Mediterranean, in a plain encircled by wooded mountains. The old name of the town, whose origins go back to antiquity, was Mylasa. The art of rug-making has been known there for centuries, and the design and colours of Milas rugs have not undergone any important modifications for more than a hundred years.

The *mihrab*, with the upper part of its niche narrowed, is typical of Milas prayer rugs; it always has a brick-red ground. The top of the arch is surmounted by a flowering tree of life, which is framed by four rose bushes in flower.

In addition to the form and colour of the *mihrab* with its floral pattern, the yellow colour of the main border of stylized carnations is also characteristic of Milas rugs; very broad in relation to the field, the border is separated from the latter by a series of small, diagonal, multi-coloured bands. On the outer edge, two serrated lines surround a band decorated with various octagonal motifs.

Turkish knot: 68 knots per sq. inch (105,000 per sq. metre)
7.5 knots per inch width (30 per 10 cm width)
9 knots per inch length (35 per 10 cm length)

Pl. 21 KIRSEHIR

(Anatolia) 1940
Dimensions: 67 × 37 inches (170 × 95 cm)

The town of Kirsehir, with a population of 20,000 inhabitants, lies 118 miles from Ankara in the direction of Kayseri. In the fourteenth and fifteenth centuries it was the spiritual centre of the powerful Moslem sect of the Ahis, certain of whose members occupied important positions such as that of governor of the province. It is rare for the pious Moslem to pray upon a rug with a *mihrab*. The production of prayer rugs is especially intended for the Western clientele.

In this example, the *mihrab*, in a fine red, has an upper part in steps, crowned with a motif of double latch-hooks. The whole circumference of the field is bordered by a row of small stylized carnations. The prayer arch stands out against a blue ground scattered with little touches of red; the flower beds set above and below are identical.

In the principal border, tulips and stylized cypresses are arranged in regular fashion. On either side, a narrow band precedes a small border having a floral pattern on a white ground.

Turkish knot: 79 knots per sq. inch (122,400 per sq. metre)

   8.5 knots per inch width (34 per 10 cm width)

   9 knots per inch length (36 per 10 cm length)

Warp: four strands of wool

Double weft: of red wool

Pile: single strand of wool of medium fineness

12 colours: 3 reds, 3 blues, 1 yellow, 1 brown, 1 brownish black, 1 beige, 1 green 1 white

Pl. 22   CAL

(Anatolia) *circa* 1930

Dimensions: 70 × 46 inches (178 × 118 cm)

Turkish knot: 64 knots per sq. inch (99,200 per sq. metre)

   8 knots per inch width (31 per 10 cm width)

   8 knots per inch length (32 per 10 cm length)

Warp: two strands of wool

Double weft: of grey wool

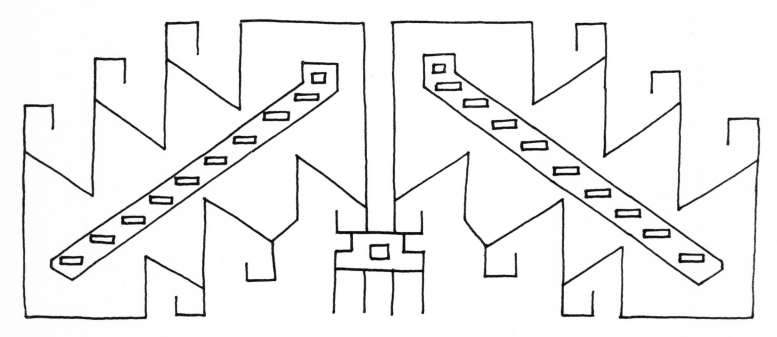

Pile: two strands of wool of medium thickness, slightly washed

8 colours (faded in parts by the light): 3 reds, 2 yellows, 1 mauve, 1 white, 1 brownish black

Cal is a village which has only a small carpet production. It is situated at a distance of 62 miles from Ushak, towards Denizli.

The field of the example shown is occupied largely by a hexagon with a red ground, bordered inside by a half-serrated and half-stepped line and outside by a band of small repeated motifs. At the top and bottom, a row of latch-hooks are terminated by a variant of the diamond-shaped motif called *mahi-tu-huse*, which stands out against the yellow ground that is edged with six multicoloured stepped lines. The central serrated motif encloses another lozenge of elongated shape crossed by two lateral bars. A large motif made up of stylized leaves decorates the grey ground of each of the corners.

Around the field is a pretty band of stylized carnations, found again outside the main border, which is decorated with pairs of leaves with latch-hooks and accentuated by two small serrated bands.

The dominant yellow colour gives this carpet a rather unusual appearance.

Pl. 23 SIVAS

(Anatolia) 1920
Dimensions: 79 × 58 inches (200 × 148 cm)

Turkish knot: 88 knots per sq. inch (136,000 per sq. metre)

    8.5 knots per inch width (34 per 10 cm width)

    10 knots per inch length (40 per 10 cm length)

Warp: three strands of natural beige wool

Double weft: of natural brown wool

Pile: two strands of wool of medium thickness

12 colours: 3 reds, 3 blues, 2 greens, 1 grey, 1 white, 1 brownish orange, 1 brownish black

In the Roman period, Sivas, which was then called Sebastia, was an important commercial metropolis. As early as the second century, Christianity took root there, and in the fourth century, under Licinius, the Christian community of the town paid a heavy tribute of martyrs to the new faith. But after the Turkoman conquest in 1400, the town lost its importance.

In modern times its development has only begun since the construction of the railway linking Ankara to Erzurum and Samsun. Today Sivas is an industrial town of 94,000 inhabitants that has completely abandoned the tradition of making fine carpets, which was formerly held in high honour. Even trading in carpets has lapsed there; at the very most one finds an occasional furniture salesman offering a meagre choice of coarsely knotted pieces. Formerly, Sivas rugs, whether the work of independent craftsmen or factory-made, were renowned for their fineness and good workmanship.

The prayer rug reproduced here belongs to the coarsely knotted type. It is a most attractive piece, having a *mihrab* bordered with latch-hooks that enclose a rather elaborate motif in the arch of the niche. The two flower beds have the same pattern of stylized pomegranates; flowers and little stars fill the corner above the prayer niche. A similar little floral strip surrounds the flower beds, the field and the two borders. The inner one is decorated with carnations, and the outer one with pomegranates.

Pl. 24 HEREKE

Late 19th century
Dimensions: 69 × 49 inches (174 × 125 cm)
Turkish knot: 379 knots per sq. inch (588,00 per sq. metre)
   17 knots per inch width (70 per 10 cm width)
   21 knots per inch length (84 per 10 cm length)
Warp: two strands of natural silk
Double weft: of beige cotton
Pile: two strands of natural silk
14 colours: 3 reds, 3 browns, 3 blues, 1 white, 2 yellows, 1 green, 1 beige

The ancient city of Ancyrona, where Constantine the Great died in 337, was situated on the site of Hereke, set inside a bay of the Gulf of Izmit, 42 miles from Istanbul. Hereke is renowned for the beauty of the carpets it produces. The factory was established by the sultans, who had luxurious early models made there, of extreme fineness.

In this example, which dates from the end of the nineteenth century, the whole field is covered with lozenge shapes decorated with flowers.

Arranged in the very wide principal border, flanked by two sets of three small bands, are some extremely beautiful vases of flowers. The photograph is unable to reproduce exactly the delicacy of the design, particularly the silky reflections of the pile, which vary with the light. The overall impression is light and elegant, proof of the perfection attained by Hereke rugs.

IRAN

Pl. 25   SHIRAZ

Fars, 1979 according to the date in the carpet, but probably more recent
Dimensions: 106 × 73 inches (268 × 186 cm)

Persian knot: 51 knots per sq. inch (78,400 per sq. metre)
  7 knots per inch width (28 per 10 cm width)
  7 knots per inch length (28 per 10 cm length)
Warp: two strands of natural greyish black goat's hair)
Double weft: of natural dark goat's hair
Pile: two strands of wool, chemically washed
7 colours: 2 reds, 2 blues, 1 brown, 1 white, 1 brownish black

The carpets known under the name of Shiraz all come from the neighbouring villages, for there are no looms in the town itself. They are characterized, as in the example reproduced, by a field of varying degrees of darkness, decorated with three medallions or with a large hexagon. The warp and weft threads of goat's hair or wool give these rugs more suppleness than those made on a cotton warp and weft.

The field is covered with bunches of flowers, four of which (in white) stand out particularly. At both ends, one can read the date of the year it was woven, 1338 of the Hegira, repeated four times, this date is also featured on the reverse.

Entirely encircled by a serrated line, the field is bordered by nine bands of various widths which, starting from the inside working outwards, are as follows: a white dotted line, a variation of the Caucasian wine-glass border, a band of *boteh* motifs, a little band of slanting stripes on either side of the main border, which itself is patterned with roses, a band of small *boteh* motifs and two spotted bands.

Though there are no stylized animals in this example, they are commonly used as decorative motifs in carpets of this type.

Pl. 26 KERMAN-AFSHAR

(Kerman region) 1970
Dimensions: 83 × 59 inches (212 × 154 cm)
Persian knot: 91 knots per sq. inch (140,800 per sq. metre)

8 knots per inch width (32 per 10 cm width)
11 knots per inch length (44 per 10 cm length)
Warp: four strands of undyed cotton
Double weft: of red cotton
Pile: two strands of wool of medium thickness, chemically washed
8 coulurs: 2 reds, 2 blues, 1 white, 1 brown, 1 orange, 1 green

One can distinguish two sorts of Afshar rugs, those from the region of Niriz (Shiraz) and those from the region of Kerman (Sirjan and Bam). In Europe the latter are called Kerman-Afshar, in order to place them more correctly geographically speaking.

The design of this carpet is called *panj gole Parizi*, that is to say, five flowers from the village of Pariz. If it were not for this designation, one would hardly guess that the five medallions that adorn the field of this piece represent flowers. The three bands of the same width that form the border are also patterned with floral motifs. The overall impression of great simplicity does not lack charm.

Pl. 27 KERMAN

1970
Dimensions: 157 × 115 inches (400 × 292 cm)
Persian knot: 201 knots per sq. inch (312,000 per sq. metre)
15 knots per inch width (60 per 10 cm width)
13 knots per inch length (52 per 10 cm length)
Warp: twelve strands of undyed cotton

Double weft: four strands of blue cotton
Pile: two strands of fine wool
14 colours in soft shades: 3 reds, 3 blues, 3 beiges,
2 greens, 2 browns, 1 white

The cartoon for this carpet is the work of an accomplished artist: the design called Shah Abbas, from the

name of the seventeenth-century ruler who patronized the rug-making art, consists of an elegant central medallion composed of several medallions superimposed upon the oval field of the red ground. The floral decoration of the latter is of exquisite delicacy and forms a harmonious combination with that of the corners and principal border. The fourteen colours are particularly beautiful and well chosen.

Pl. 28 KALAR DASHTI

1970
Dimensions: 100 × 70 inches (254 × 178 cm)
Turkish knot: 49 knots per sq. inch (75,400 per sq. metre)
   6.5 knots per inch width (26 per 10 cm width)
   7 knots per inch length (29 per 10 cm length)
Warp: six strands of undyed cotton
Double weft: of natural brown wool
Pile: two strands of wool of average thickness
9 coulours: 2 reds, 2 blues, 1 white, 1 yellow, 1 brown, 1 orange, 1 brownish black

The plain of Kalar (Kalar Dasht) owes its name to Mount Kalar. It dominates a verdant valley reached by Marzanabad, which is to be found on the Karaja-Chalus road. About 10 miles of mountainous road separate Marzanabad from the entrance to the valley, situated at an altitude of about 6,550 feet. Rug manufacture is carried on in almost all villages of the valley, especially at Kalino, Rudbar and Makulud, with the exception of Hassan Kif, the administrative centre.

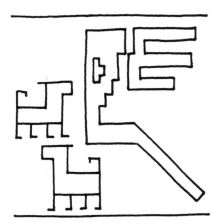

Designs on the Kalar Dashti rug are mainly of the *jangali* (of the jungle) and *majmei* types. Rug production here is not of long standing, since it goes back only fifty years.

Another curiosity of Kalar Dasht is that the weavers work in the open air. The vertical looms are in fact mounted against the façades of the houses, under the eaves. In bad weather the weavers cover the tops of the looms with a sheet of plastic, to prevent the rug and the warp threads from becoming wet.

With its broad style and the large hexagonal motif on a red ground decorated with two *sandugh* motifs, each containing a samovar, this example recalls the rugs of the Caucasus. The small diamond-shaped motif in the centre and at each end of the hexagon is called *pialeh*, and the white zigzag line that borders the hexagon is called *karim khani*.

The absence of axial symmetry is striking; the animals (goats and dogs) are all arranged in the same direction, whether on the field or in the principal border, which also includes *kadradomes* (stylized foxes). On either side of the latter are bands with floral motifs of different colours.

Pl. 29 KARAJA

(Azerbaijan) 1970
Dimensions: 77 × 55 inches (195 × 139 cm)
Turkish knot: 69 knots per sq. inch (106,400 per sq. metre)
   7 knots per inch width (28 per 10 cm width)
   9.5 knots per inch length (38 per 10 cm length)
Warp: seven strands of undyed cotton
Single weft: of blue cotton
Pile: two strands of wool of medium thickness, chemically washed
12 colours: 3 reds, 3 blues, 2 yellows, 1 white, 1 pink, 1 brownish black, 1 beige

Karaja is a small mountain village near Shahsavar, which lies on the road between Tabriz and Ahar. It is difficult to reach; there is no access by road. Its rugs have a

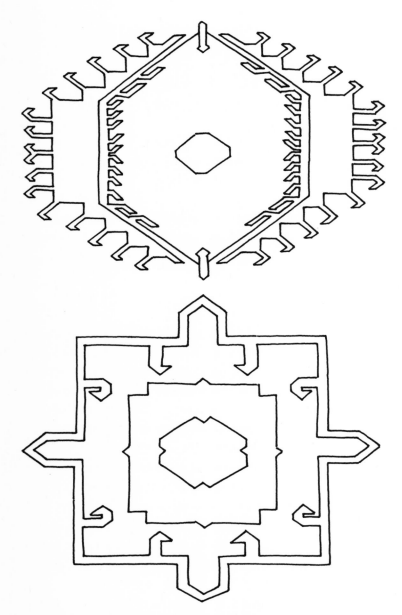

Heriz or Mehriban types; here the warp threads are single and the motifs smaller and more delicate.

The red ground of the field is patterned with stylized trees, leaves and flowers. Of the three medallions, two are square-shaped with four little bars. These also have floral decoration and, in each corner, a stylized scorpion. The central medallion is a hexagon encircled by latch-hooks. Three little stripes surround the central floral border.

The style is simple; good quality wool gives the carpets of this region great strength.

Pl. 30 MIR

1970
Dimensions: 146 × 97 inches (371 × 273 cm)
Persian knot: 103 knots per sq. inch (159,600 per sq. metre)
   9.5 knots per inch width (38 per 10 cm width)
   10.5 knots per inch length (42 per 10 cm length)
Warp: twelve strands of undyed cotton
Double weft: of blue cotton
Pile: two strands of wool of medium fineness, chemically washed
9 colours: 2 reds, 2 blues, 2 yellows, 1 brown, 1 white, 1 beige

The *boteh-miri* motif depicted in this carpet is an old pattern that originated in India. Here is the form used by the weavers of Mir, a village of the Burujird region. A tiny seed-plot of *botehs* covers the whole field, which

character all their own, different from those of other production centres of the region, which belong to the

Pl. 31 SAROUK

(Arak region) 1970
Dimensions: 122 × 86 inches (310 × 219 cm)
Persian knot: 119 knots per sq. inch (184,800 per sq. metre)
    10.5 knots per inch width (42 per 10 cm width)
    11 knots per inch length (44 per 10 cm length)
Warp: nine strands of undyed cotton
Double weft: of blue cotton
Pile: two strands of rather fine wool, chemically washed
10 colours: 3 reds, 3 blues, 1 green, 1 white, 1 brownish black, 1 yellow

Sarouk rugs are made throughout the region of Arak, especially in Arak itself, at Khonsar and Mahalat, and not only at Sarouk as their name might lead one to suppose. Well known since about 1870, they have an excellent reputation for solidity. The weavers of the region are accustomed to working after a pattern and can thus vary their designs.

In this example of classical style, the richness of the motifs and the skill of their arrangement strikes one immediately: the central rosette blends perfectly with the graceful tracery that links the flowers of every species that cover the field. An additional note of elegance is given by the rounding of the corners of the blue ground.

This field is framed by a main border of flowery arabesques, accentuated on each side by two narrow floral bands.

has a golden ground in this example, although more often the ground is red.

Its many very fine borders give this carpet an unusual air. The principal band is also decorated with the *boteh-miri* pattern, this time of more elongated form.

A feeling of restful delicacy emanates from this rug. Today as in the past, this type of rug is highly coveted.

Pl. 32 YALAMEH

(Aliabad, Isfahan region) 1970
Dimensions: 120 × 85 inches (305 × 215 cm)
Persian knot: 87 knots per sq. inch (135,000 per sq. metre)
   7.5 knots per inch width (30 per 10 cm width)
   11 knots per inch length (45 per 10 cm length)
Warp: natural grey and brown wool, one strand of each colour twisted together
Double weft: two strands of natural brown wool
Pile: two strands of wool of medium thickness
8 colours: 2 reds, 2 blues, 1 white, 1 grey, 1 brown, 1 beige

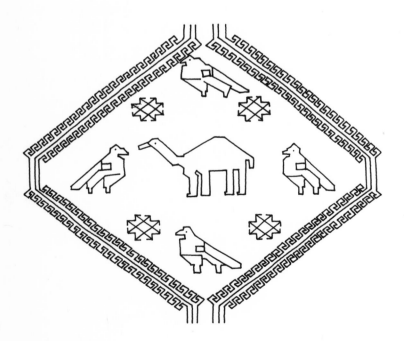

The rug reproduced has a main border with a white ground, encircled by narrower borders, and a field with a black ground, upon which are arranged four white hexagonal medallions, interlinked and bordered in red. The motifs in the central medallions include a camel, four birds and stylized flowers; the motifs in the medallions at the ends have sheep (?), chickens and mice (?), in addition to a camel and stylized flowers. The outline of the medallions and the red framework are trimmed with a double row of latch-hooks of Caucasian origin, as are the little eight-pointed stars of the inner band, edged (on the side nearest the field) by a line of red latch-hooks. The field is embellished with animals, birds, crosses and closed latch-hooks.

On both sides of the principal border, two small bands are to be found with interesting motifs: the triangle, formerly a symbol of divinity, and the motif underneath—of Chinese origin—called 'thunder border'. The latch-hook motifs of the main band are reminiscent of those on Yomud rugs from Turkestan.

Everything about this carpet points to influences from the Caucasus and Turkestan. The simplicity of the geometric shapes and the appealing gaiety of the colours make it an attractive piece.

Pl. 33 ISFAHAN

1960
Dimensions: 78 × 49 inches (198 × 124 cm)
Persian knot: 414 knots per sq. inch (640,000 per sq. metre)

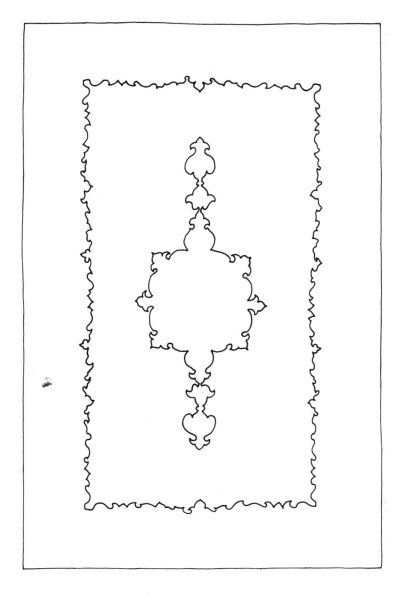

Double weft: of blue cotton
Pile: two strands of very fine wool, chemically washed
12 colours: 3 reds, 3 whites, 1 yellow, 1 gold, 1 green, 1 white, 1 beige, 1 brown

Today the rugs of Isfahan are among the finest to be found in Iran. Their prices are therefore high, as are those of Nain rugs, which are of a closely related type.

The decoration of this piece uses the traditional floral motifs that already figured in seventeenth-century rugs and in the early ceramics of the mosques. The design of the central medallion, square-shaped with graceful projections, and that of the motifs set in the corners is evidence of much careful thought.

Like the field, the three bands of the border are patterned with flowers among which one can recognize roses, tulips and daisies. The two bands with blue grounds are narrower than the red one, and none of them have rectilinear sides.

One can scracely imagine the patience necessary to create such a lovely example. Usually women and children are employed for this type of work, sometimes carried out under difficult conditions.

Pl. 34   QUM

1960
Dimensions: 138 × 95 inches (351 × 242 cm)
Persian knot: 232 knots per sq. inch (360,000 per sq. metre)
   15 knots per inch width (60 per 10 cm width)
   15 knots per inch length (60 per 10 cm length)

20 knots per inch width (80 per 10 cm width)
20 knots per inch length (80 per 10 cm length)
Warp: three strands of silk

Warp: unbleached cotton
Weft: unbleached cotton
Pile: wool
12 colours: 2 greens, 2 reds, 2 blues, 2 yellows,
1 orange, 1 beige, 1 white, 1 black

The composition of the classical rugs of the seventeenth century has inspired the good-quality pieces produced at Qum. The one shown is no exception.

The floral decoration of the field contrasts very pleasantly with the delicate green ground, a colour rarely used in carpets. The border, with its arabesques, completes the success of the whole and shows the high degree of skill reached in this holy city that has a relatively recent tradition of carpet-making.

Pl. 35   KASHGAI

(Shiraz region) 1960
Dimensions: 89 × 51 inches (227 × 129 cm)
Persian knot: 90 knots per sq. inch (140,400 per sq. metre)
   9 knots per inch width (36 per 10 cm width)
   10 knots per inch length (39 per 10 cm length)
Warp: two strands of goat's hair, one brown and one undyed thread twisted together
Double weft: goat's hair, one brown and one red thread
Pile: one strand of wool of medium thickness
7 colours: 2 reds, 2 blues, 1 yellow, 1 white, 1 brownish black

The Kashgai people were originally Turkish-speaking

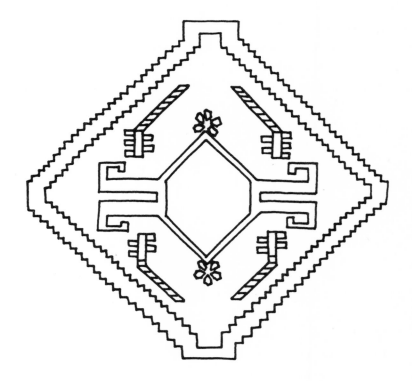

nomads who lived in Fars, that is to say, in the region of Shiraz. This is why their rugs are often referred to under the name of "Turkish Shiraz". But nowadays, a good number of the now sedentary Kashgai race have settled in the villages of the region. The have, however, retained their habit of knotting their carpets on the horizontal looms of the nomads. In fine weather one sees women working on them in the garden or in the courtyard in front of the house.

The field here is a large hexagon, inside which one finds a number of motifs in the form of leaves, notched on one side, and flowers. The diamond-shaped central medallion is encircled by two lines, the inner one jagged and the outer one cut in steps. In the middle of the medallion is a hexagon ornamented with two large lateral latch-hooks and with a flower at two points. Four jagged motifs frame a big flower in each corner.

Stars decorate the principal border, which is flanked by two bands, one narrower than the other.

Pl. 36 KASHAN

1960
Dimensions: 97 × 61 inches (246 × 155 cm)
Persian knot: 274 knots per sq. inch (422,400 per sq. metre)
    16 knots per inch width (64 per 10 cm width)
    16.5 knots per inch length (66 per 10 cm length)
Warp: three strands of fine undyed cotton
Double weft: two strands of blue cotton
Pile: two strands of fine wool with silky sheen, accentuated by chemical treatment
12 colours: 3 reds, 3 blues, 2 greens, 1 yellow, 1 orange, 1 white, 1 brownish black

Kashan, a town renowned for its textiles, produces rugs of exceptional quality. The famous carpet from the mosque at Ardebil, now in the Victoria and Albert Museum in London, is the work of a Kashan weaver. Even though some experts cast doubt upon its place of origin, it is probable that it was woven in that town.

The example we reproduce has a pattern of extraordinary richness. Certainly designed by an artist of talent, it reminds one of the carpets of the great seventeenth-century period. The border, with stylized flowers

(predominantly in blues of various shades), surrounds the fine red field which is richly decorated with floral tracery. The interlinked corner pieces repeat and develop the motifs of the border without a break. The different bands of the border cannot be clearly defined, since the motifs of the central strip encroach upon the adjacent ones.

All the lines of the pattern, simultaneously graceful and vigorous, converge on the central medallion. This almost circular form has two lengthwise projections and is decorated with formalized vases and flowers in a very varied range of colours. The virtuousity of the design is enhanced by the skillful use of twelve different colours. This very beautiful piece is evidence that Iran still produces rugs of high quality.

Pl. 37 BIJAR

(Kurdistan, Garrus) 1960
Dimensions: 145 × 90 inches (368 × 268 cm)
Turkish knot: 112 knots per sq. inch (174,000 per sq. metre)
   11.5 knots per inch width (46 per 10 cm width)
   9.5 knots per inch length (38 per 10 cm length)
Warp: unbleached cotton
Double weft: brown and unbleached cotton
Pile: wool
10 colours: 2 reds, 2 blues, 2 greens, 1 white, 1 yellow, 1 beige, 1 brownish black

The first impression received from this rug is that the craftsman went to great pains to achieve a completely regular design of small motifs. Nevertheless he did not lack imagination, and if one looks more closely, one can find stylized birds between the flowers and leaves. The

central and corner motifs are very graceful, and the border shows the classical decoration of Bijar.

Pl. 38 KOLIAYEH

(Kurdistan) 1960
Dimensions: 92 × 58 inches (234 × 148 cm)
Turkish knot: 64 knots per sq. inch (99,000 per sq. metre)
   7.5 knots per inch width (30 per 10 cm width)
   8 knots per inch length (33 per 10 cm length)

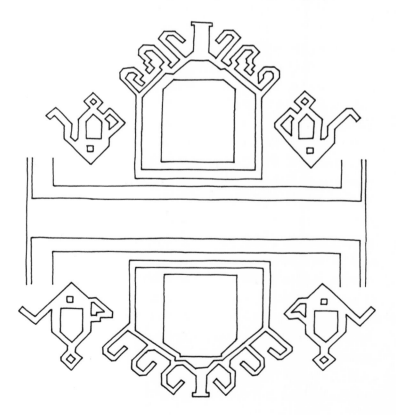

Single warp: twelve strands of fine undyed cotton
Weft: four strands of red cotton
Pile: two strands of wool of medium thickness, chemically washed
12 colours: 3 reds, 3 blues, 2 browns, 1 white, 1 yellow, 1 green, 1 grey

This is a carpet from Iranian Kurdistan, which in construction bears more resemblance to Hamadan rugs than to the rugs of its own region.

The geometric style of the design recalls the Kazak rugs of the Caucasus. Its Persian name of *takhteh jamshid* ("throne of the King"), is derived from the double central motif. The principal border, with a white ground, is divided lengthwise into compartments by wide red bands (except for one in blue), trimmed with two small motifs and a large double latch-hook, between which are depicted stylized trees. Across the width of the carpet these bands are replaced by rosettes alternating with formalized animals. This border is enclosed by two narrow bands, the outer one consisting only of rosettes, and the inner one of rosettes and dots. The latter is separated from the field by a band with a yellow ground, patterned with rosettes, between which meanders an unbroken line.

The field has a dark blue ground with large geometric motifs. The red central part—with stylized ewers and lines with latch-hooks—is evocative of Kazak rugs; however, the wool and the weave are different, the Koliayeh rug being woven on a single warp and in a softer wool than a Kazak rug.

The charm of this rug lies in the very warm shades employed and in the richness of the colour range.

Pl. 39 ARDEBIL

(Azerbaijan) 1960
Dimensions: 111 × 43 inches (282 × 110 cm)
Turkish knot: 107 knots per sq. inch (165,600 per sq. metre)
   9 knots per inch width (36 per 10 cm width)
   11.5 knots per inch length (46 per 10 cm length)
Warp: five strands, four in cotton and one in goat's hair
Double weft: undyed cotton
Pile: wool of medium thickness, chemically treated to tone down the colours and to make then glossy
10 colours: 2 reds, 2 blues, 2 yellows, 1 white, 1 brown, 1 brownish black, 1 beige

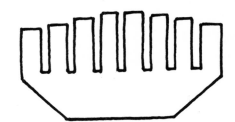

It is at Ardebil, a large town of 90,000 inhabitants situated at an altitude of 3,600 feet to the east of the ancient extinct volcano of Kuh-i-Savalan that, according to tradition, Zoroastra wrote the *Avesta* ("law").

In the northwest of the town stands the mausoleum of the holy man Sheikh Safi al-Din Ishaq, who died in 1334. Nadir Shah, who founded the Afshar dynasty, was crowned at Ardebil in 1736.

The geometric decoration of this carpet is of the same style as that of Caucasian rugs: many double latch-hooks, flowers, combs, dogs and trees of life. The principal border, decorated with crosses and rosettes, is encircled by two narrow bands.

The Ardebil rug is distinguished from the Caucasian rug by its knotting and by its less lustrous wool.

Pl. 40 SARAB

(Azerbaijan) 1960
Dimensions: 85 × 37 inches (215 × 94 cm)
Turkish knot: 49 knots per sq. inch (75,900 per sq. metre)
   6 knots per inch width (23 per 10 cm width)
   8 knots per inch length (33 per 10 cm length)
Warp: three strands of natural wool
Double weft: natural beige wool
Pile: two strands of rather thick wool
8 colours: 2 reds, 2 blues, 1 green, 1 white, 1 yellow, 1 brown

Sarab, a small place in the Ardebil region, is known for its rugs of elongated shape and heavy quality, the design of which varies little. Large medallions cover the field, which usually has a beige ground or, less frequently, a red one, as is the case here. The three hexagonal medallions in the field enclose a second hexagon, ornamented with latch-hooks and flowers. At both ends are triangular motifs resembling pendants.

The border includes two bands, one decorated with stylized pomegranates, the other with a white ground and having large and small squares surrounded by latch-hooks. A row of sugar-loaves runs around the outside and alongside the field.

Pl. 41 MISHKIN

(Azerbaijan, Mishkinshahr) 1950
Dimensions: 111 × 52 inches (283 × 132 cm)
Turkish knot: 65 knots per sq. inch (100,800 per sq. metre)
   7 knots per inch width (28 per 10 cm width)
   9 knots per inch length (36 per 10 cm length)
Warp: five strands of undyed cotton
Double weft: grey cotton
Pile: two strands of wool of average thickness
12 colours: 3 reds, 3 blues, 2 yellows, 1 white, 1 brown, 1 green, 1 brownish black

The small settlement of Mishkinshahr (formerly Khiov) lies about 6,000 feet above sea level at the foot of the

Kuh-i-Savalan. The decoration of its rugs, which enjoy high repute, remind one of Caucasian carpets.

Two floral zigzag bands are arranged on the dark red ground of the field forming five diamond shapes of large size, inside each of which four joined triangles form another diamond shape, with a jagged border that is furnished with eight small latch-hooks. A little black denticulated line encircles the field. The frame includes floral bands, separated from each other by a small dotted line.

This is a fine piece, rather restrained in design, but with numerous colours blended with confident taste.

Pl. 42 BIRJAND

(Khorassan) 1950
Dimensions: 89 × 57 inches (226 × 144 cm)
Persian knot: 418 knots per sq. inch (648,000 per sq. metre)
  18 knots per inch width (72 per 10 cm width)
  23 knots per inch length (90 per 10 cm length)
Warp: unbleached cotton
Double weft: unbleached cotton
Pile: wool and silk
14 colours: 3 reds, 3 blues, 3 greens, 1 pink, 1 beige, 1 orange, 1 white, 1 brownish black

The design of the rug shown here is not in the usual style of Birjand. The lines of the field, which is filled in with medallions, are very elegant and show a high standard of decorative refinement. This piece, which

owes its brilliance to the use of silk, is completed by a border that harmonizes well with the field.

Pl. 43 VARAMIN

1950
Dimensions: 108 × 83 inches (320 × 210 cm)
Persian knot: 194 knots per sq. inch (300,000 per sq. metre)
  15 knots per inch width (60 per 10 cm width)
  13 knots per inch length (50 per 10 cm length)
Warp: unbleached cotton
Double weft: blue cotton
Pile: wool
8 colours: 2 reds, 2 blues, 1 brown, 1 white, 1 yellow, 1 green

Varamin is situated 26 miles away from Teheran. To reach it one passes through the ancient city of Rayy. After Rayy, on the south side of the rocky spur which blocks the Teheran plain, one can distinguish several *Imamzadas* ("shrines"), and the tomb of Bibi Shahrbanu. According to tradition Bibi Shahrbanu was the daughter of Yezdigird III, the last Sassanian king, and wife of Imam Hussein. Only women are allowed to enter into the mausoleum.

The Varamin rugs, like this one, usually have a blue ground and a uniform design of flowers in a pattern called *minakhani* ("daisy"), which origintaed in Kurdistan and was to be found already in the last century on Bijar rugs. The border on this type of rug is also unchanging.

Pl. 44   TAFRESH

1950
Dimensions: 76 × 54 inches (193 × 137 cm)
Turkish knot: 90 knots per sq. inch (140,000 per sq. metre)
    10 knots per inch width (40 per 10 cm width)
    9 knots per inch length (35 per 10 cm length)
Warp: unbleached cotton
Single weft: unbleached cotton
Pile: wool
10 colours: 2 reds, 2 blues, 1 pink, 1 yellow, 1 orange, 1 green, 1 white, 1 brownish black

The large village of Tafresh is reached via the minor road from Arak to Saveh and lies at a distance of 57 miles from Arak. Rugs made here are of an uncommon type, knotted with a single weft (consequently the two loops forming the knot are visible on the reverse side); their colouring is generally gayer than that of rugs from the neighbouring regions of Hamadan. Another characteristic of these Tafresh rugs lies in the composition of the central medallion, a feature that appears very frequently.

Pl. 45   NAIN

1940
Dimensions: 170 × 129 inches (431 × 328 cm)
Persian knot: 372 knots per sq. inch (576,000 per sq. metre)
    20 knots per inch width (80 per 10 cm width)
    18 knots per inch length (72 per 10 cm length)
Warp: raw silk
Double weft: blue cotton
Pile: wool
12 colours: 3 reds, 3 blues, 1 yellow, 1 green, 1 brown, 1 beige, 1 white, 1 black

Before they were knotting rugs, the Nain workers were occupied in the weaving of fine clothing known as *aba*, which almost disappeared with the arrival of Western fashion. Because of this they were obliged to turn their talent to rug-making. Since they were used to working with fine thread, they produced very fine rugs right from the start, and their reputation spread rapidly.

    This is a harmonious example with a design that has become typical of the region. At the centre of the cream-coloured field is a very handsome medallion. The border with its arabesques pleasantly surrounds the field, and the warm colouring shows the skill of the maker of this rug.

Pl. 46   HERIZ

(Azerbaijan) 1940
Dimensions: 142 × 106 inches (360 × 268 cm)
Turkish knot: 64 knots per sq. inch (98,600 per sq. metre)
    7 knots per inch width (29 per 10 cm width)
    8.5 knots per inch length (34 per 10 cm length)
Warp: unbleached cotton

Double weft: blue cotton
Pile: wool
12 colours: 3 reds, 2 blues, 2 yellows, 2 browns,
1 brownish black, 1 green, 1 white

Although the rounded corners of the design link this
rug with the Tabriz patterns, the construction is certainly
typical of Heriz in its density and in the very compact
knot—features that are greatly appreciated in the West.
The border bears a pattern characteristic of seventeenth-
century rugs, carefully and accurately detailed. The
white spandrels add a note of gaiety and successfully
complete the effect.

Pl. 47 LURISTAN

1940
Dimensions: 116 × 60 inches (295 × 152 cm)
Turkish knot: 59 knots per sq. inch (91,800 per
sq. metre)
   7 knots per inch width (27 per 10 cm width)
   8.5 knots per inch length (34 per 10 cm length)
Warp: two strands of natural beige-brown wool
Single weft: natural brown wool
Pile: two strands of wool of medium thickness
10 colours: 3 reds, 2 blues, 1 white, 1 yellow, 1 green,
1 orange, 1 brownish black

Luristan rugs are made by the Lur tribes, who still live
partly as nomads. The region lies on the frontier with
Iraq.

On the blue-black ground of the field, we find diverse large stylized motifs—willows, cypresses, roses, tulips—all arranged in the same direction. In the main border, cruciform motifs alternate with two birds facing one another. Two floral-patterned hands, one with a white ground, the other yellow, complete the border. The design is simple, giving an impression of a primitive but captivating art.

Pl. 48   BALUCHI

(Mashhad region, Turbat-i-Haidari) 1940
Dimensions: 64 × 34 inches (164 × 85 cm)
Persian knot: 148 knots per sq. inch (230,000 per sq. metre)
    11.5 knots per inch width (46 per 10 cm width)
    13 knots per inch length (50 per 10 cm length)
Warp: two strands of wool
Double weft: natural brown goat's hair
Pile: two strands of rather fine wool, with natural sheen
5 colours: 2 browns, 1 red, 1 blue, 1 white

Turbat-i-Haidari is a town of some 20,000 inhabitants, situated at an altitude of 4,300 feet. The best Baluchi carpets, like this example, are made in the surrounding villages. The design is extremely simple and has very few colours, which is rare in Iran, where some carpets have as many as fourteen colours.

The field is covered by two rows of large stylized flowers in light colours that alternate with the same, more subdued, motifs in red. The main border, which is very broad, includes large floral motifs linked by

bands of double latch-hooks. Between the field and the border is a double serrated line and, outside, a small zigzag border.

146

Pl. 49 MASHHAD

1935
Dimensions: 124 × 80 inches (315 × 204 cm)
Persian knot: 503 knots per sq. inch (780,000 per sq. metre)
20 knots per inch width (78 per 10 cm width)
25 knots per inch length (100 per 10 cm length)
Warp: unbleached cotton
Double weft: blue cotton
Pile: wool
14 colours: 3 reds, 3 blues, 3 greens, 1 yellow, 1 orange, 1 beige, 1 white, 1 brownish black

In this well-balanced design, beautiful flowers and arabesques, reminiscent of the seventeenth-century classical rug designs, cover the field. Note also the motif: cloudbands or stylized serpents. The borders are multiple, finely designed and in perfect harmony with the field.

The signature of the Emogli Factory figures in a cartouche inserted into the exterior border. Through its perfection of technique, this rug holds its own with the best productions of past and present.

Pl. 50 MASLAGHAN

(Nobaran, Maslaghan, Saveh district) 1930
Dimensions: 77 × 53 inches (196 × 135 cm)
Turkish knot: 108 knots per sq. inch (168,000 per sq. metre)
10.5 knots per inch width (42 per 10 cm width)
10 knots per inch length (40 per 10 cm length)
Warp: unbleached cotton
Single weft: unbleached cotton
Pile: wool
8 colours: 2 reds, 2 blues, 2 browns, 1 white, 1 yellow

There are a number of villages in the Saveh district where good carpets are made. The best known is Nobaran, to the east of Dergezin and about 37 miles from Saveh on the road going towards Hamadan. The Nobaran rugs are mostly sold in the market of this locality. They have a very special style of their own that one can spot among thousands: the field is bordered by two zigzag lines that are repeated in reverse on the borders of the medallion and right up to the projections of the lozenge.

Pl. 51 SEMNAN

1930
Dimensions: 176 × 124 inches (446 × 314 cm)
Persian knot: 280 knots per sq. inch (434,000 per sq. metre)
16 knots per inch width (62 per 10 cm width)
18 knots per inch length (70 per 10 cm length)
Warp: unbleached cotton
Double weft: blue cotton
Pile: wool
14 colours: 3 reds, 3 blues, 3 greens, 1 beige, 1 white, 1 orange, 1 yellow, 1 brownish black

The important town of Semnan, which lies 136 miles from Teheran, dates from the Sassanian period. In 1036, it was pillaged by gangs of Turks who massacred part of the population, but it was rebuilt ten years afterwards. Later it suffered invasions by the Mongols and by Timurid troops; however, as it represented an important halting place on the road to Mashhad, the town was always built up again.

There was never a great output of carpets from Semnan, but they have always been conspicuous by their quality. The one we reproduce is proof of this. The triple border and the medallions are of remarkably fine design, and the execution is perfect. It is a pity that the artist did not sign his work.

Pl. 52   INJILAS

(Hamadan region) 1920
Dimensions: 76 × 61 inches (192 × 154 cm)
Turkish knot: 77 knots per sq. inch (120,000 per sq. metre)
   7.5 knots per inch width (30 per 10 cm width)
   10 knots per inch length (40 per 10 cm length)
Warp: unbleached cotton
Single weft: blue cotton
Pile: wool
8 colours: 2 reds, 2 blues, 1 green, 1 yellow, 1 white, 1 brown

Injilas is situated to the south of Hamadan at the foot of Mount Alwand, and it has been well known for a long time for the quality of its carpets and the pride of its inhabitants. One can attribute only two designs—the *boteh-miri* and the *herati*, which are reproduced here—to

this town. Serrated leaves surround lozenges with a central flower. The decoration is identical to that of ancient Feraghan rugs. Today this design is no longer used, and the Injilas rugs invariably show the *boteh-miri* motifs.

Pl. 53   ISFAHAN

Circa 1920
Dimensions: 81 × 58 inches (205 × 148 cm)
Persian knot: 361 knots per sq. inch (561,000 per sq. metre)

19.5 knots per inch width (78 per 10 cm width)
18.5 knots per inch length (72 per 10 cm length)
Warp: three strands of unbleached cotton
Weft: four strands of blue cotton
Pile: two strands of wool
14 colours: 2 reds, 1 pink, 3 blues, 2 greens, 1 orange, 2 browns, 1 yellow, 1 beige, 1 white

Isfahan had a reputation for producing great artists as long ago as the reign of Shah Abbas (1587–1628), and today it is still the artistic centre of Iran. Although the carpets produced there nowadays are not as magnificent as those made during the Golden Age, they are still very beautiful.

The weaver must have followed a cartoon when making the rug we illustrate, it is inconceivable that a carpet with a design of such precision and fineness could be the work of a craftsman who merely reproduced traditional motifs from memory. We are presented with a garden in full bloom, containing graceful arabesques, emphasized by the dark blue of the ground. The wide main border, in red, is also decorated with arabesques and bouquets of flowers. This very appealing rug bears witness to the highly developed artistic skill of its creator.

Pl. 54   JOSHAGAN

(Isfahan region) end of the 19th century
Dimensions: 88 × 57 inches (223 × 146 cm)
Persian knot: 232 knots per sq. inch (360,000 per sq. metre)

15 knots per inch width (60 per 10 cm width)
15 knots per inch length (60 per 10 cm length)
Warp: unbleached cotton
Double weft: blue cotton
Pile: wool
10 colours: 2 reds, 2 blues, 2 greens, 1 yellow, 1 white, 1 orange, 1 brownish black

At one time this type of rug was the exclusive product of the village of Joshagan, but today it is also made at Meymeh and at Mucheh Khourt, two villages situated on the main road to Isfahan. Since the Second World War, the rugs made there are finer than those of Joshagan, even though the latter can claim a long tradition of rug-making dating from the sixteenth century.

This design is called *jangali* ("of the jungle") because of the numerous floral motifs covering the field.

Pl. 55   TABRIZ

End of the 19th century
Dimensions: 66 × 50 inches (168 × 128 cm)
Turkish knot: 213 knots per sq. inch (330,000 per sq. metre)
14 knots per inch width (55 per 10 cm width)
15 knots per inch length (60 per 10 cm length)
Warp: unbleached cotton
Double weft: red cotton
Pile: wool
12 colours: 3 reds, 3 blues, 2 yellows, 1 white, 1 brownish black, 1 beige, 1 green

A large, elegantly shaped lozenge stands out on the floral field and encloses a most graceful medallion. Other flowers are strewn all over the borders of this Tabriz rug. By virtue of its composition as well as its colouring, this is a characteristic example of the late nineteenth and early twentieth centuries.

Pl. 56 TABRIZ (HAJJI JALIL)

End of the 19th century
Dimensions: 73 × 51 inches (186 × 130 cm)
Turkish knot: 366 knots per sq. inch (567,000 per sq. metre)
   20.5 knots per inch width (81 per 10 cm width)
   18 knots per inch length (70 per 10 cm length)
Warp: white silk
Double weft: red cotton
Pile: silk
12 colours: 3 reds, 3 blues, 1 white, 1 green, 1 grey, 1 orange, 1 brown, 1 yellow

Hajji Jalil was a well-known craftsman from Marand, a small town near Tabriz, whose fame was such that all the products of his workshop bore his name.

   This is a fine prayer rug; the *mihrab* has a red ground; its vault is supported by two graceful columns. A chain, hanging from the apex down to the centre of the prayer arch, holds a lamp decorated with flowers. Beneath this is a bouquet. At the top of the *mihrab*, the cross panel is composed of ten small vaulted compartments and, at the foot, there are nine, all adorned with garlands and arabesques.

Eight borders—seven narrow and one wide—frame the *mihrab*. They are all patterned with flowers.

Pl. 57 FERAGHAN

(Arak region) *circa* 1870
Dimensions: 81.5 × 51.5 inches (207 × 131 cm)
Turkish knot: 232 knots per sq. inch (359,100 per sq. metre)
   16 knots per inch width (63 per 10 cm width)
   14.5 knots per inch length (57 per 10 cm length)
Warp: five strands of very fine, unbleached cotton
Weft: three strands of unbleached cotton
Pile: two strands of wool
12 colours: 2 reds, 3 blues, 2 greens, 1 gold, 2 browns, 1 brownish black, 1 white

This carpet, with a design known as *Sil-i-Sultan*, was made for the prince who governed Isfahan around 1870. Its structure shows that it was woven in the region of Arak (formerly Feraghan). The field with a white ground has an all-over design of roses and other flowers found in the *Sil-i-Sultan* design, which is the name under which these carpets are most commonly sold.

Two narrow, dark blue borders flank the red main border; all three have a floral decoration.

The general impression conveyed by this typically Persian carpet is one of great delicacy. The colours are varied but soft in tone, and they have been employed with great artistry.

Pl. 58 MAHAL

(Arak region) *circa* 1870
Dimensions: 141 × 99 inches (358 × 251 cm)
Persian knot: 132 knots per sq. inch (193,600 per sq. metre)
  11.5 knots per inch width (44 per 10 cm width)
  11.5 knots per inch length (44 per 10 cm length)
Warp: eight strands of unbleached cotton
Weft: four strands of blue cotton
Pile: two strands of wool
10 colours: 2 reds, 1 pink, 3 blues, 1 green, 1 olive green, 1 gold, 1 white

In the centre of a dark blue ground covered with flowers of varying sizes is a red motif decorated with flowers and leaves. A quarter of this central motif is repeated in each corner.

The red main border is fairly wide; it also has a decoration of large and small flowers, and on either side of it is a narrow band with a gold ground.

This carpet is the work of a village craftsman, and its design and beautiful, warm and harmonious colours are quite remarkable.

Pl. 59 KASHAN

Circa 1870
Dimensions: 85 × 49.5 inches (215 × 126 cm)
Persian knot: 342 knots per sq. inch (532,000 per sq. metre)

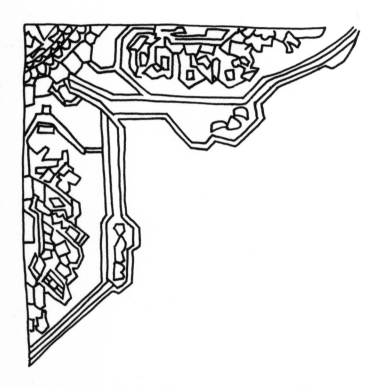

18 knots per inch width (70 per 10 cm width)
19 knots per inch length (76 per 10 cm length)
Warp: three strands of natural silk
Weft: four strands of blue cotton
Pile: two strands of natural silk
8 colours: 1 purplish red, 2 blues, 1 gold, 1 straw yellow, 1 beige, 1 brown, 1 white

This type of rug of natural silk earned for the town of Kashan its fine reputation in the nineteenth century. A polygon of a purplish red shade—the predominant colour of the rug—stands in the centre of a greyish white ground. At the heart of the polygon is a flower-shaped, sky-blue medallion. A design of linked arabesques and flowers covers the field and the corners, which are of the same purplish red shade as the polygon.

The same colour is used for the ground of the main border that is also decorated with arabesques and flowers. It is emphasized by having a narrow floral border with a sky-blue ground on each side of it. Around the outer edge of the rug and around the field, there is a narrow band of *medahil*.

The most striking feature of this rug is its purplish red colour—a very unusual one for Persian carpets.

Pl. 60 BAKHTIARI

(Village of Shalamzar, Chahar Mahal) end of the 19th century
Dimensions: 152 × 117 inches (385 × 298 cm)
Turkish knot: 95 knots per sq. inch (147,600 per sq. metre)
10 knots per inch width (41 per 10 cm width)
9 knots per inch length (36 per 10 cm length)
Warp: unbleached cotton
Double weft: unbleached cotton
Pile: wool
14 colours: 3 greens, 3 reds, 2 blues, 2 yellows, 1 orange, 1 grey, 1 brownish black, 1 black

This is a typical Bakhtiari rug, although it was made by Turkish craftsmen, immigrants to the Chahar Mahal region since the last century, which explains the Turkish knot used to make it. In its naive way the design is beautifully executed.

This "garden" pattern is often used by Tabriz factories, but it would seem that it originated in Chahar Mahal. The village of Shalamzar, where the carpet was made, has a high reputation for quality and craftsmanship.

Pl. 61 SENNEH

(Kurdistan) end of the 19th century
Dimensions: 81 × 51 inches (205 × 130 cm)
Turkish knot: 392 knots per sq. inch (608,000 per sq. metre)
   20 knots per inch width (80 per 10 cm width)
   19 knots per inch length (76 per 10 cm length)
Warp: silk in various colours
Single weft: unbleached cotton
Pile: wool
10 colours: 2 reds, 2 blues, 2 yellows, 1 pink, 1 green, 1 white, 1 brown

Two hexagonal medallions decorate the centre of the rug. The very dense sprinkling of flowers relates it to a number of other Senneh rugs, but the sustained colouring is exceptional for the period and for this type of rug.

Two small bands decorated with daisies define the border area, where leaves and flowers alternate, and the bands are linked together with arabesques.

Pl. 62 YAZD

(Kerman region) second half of the 19th century
Dimensions: 149 × 100 inches (379 × 254 cm)
Persian knot: 130 knots per sq. inch (201,600 per sq. metre)
   14 knots per inch width (56 per 10 cm width)
   9 knots per inch length (36 per 10 cm length)
Warp: unbleached cotton
Double weft: unbleached cotton
Pile: wool
10 colours: 2 reds, 2 blues, 1 yellow, 1 green, 1 beige, 1 orange, 1 white, 1 brown

Yazd has many textile factories, and its inhabitants have gained the reputation of being diligent workers. Although built in the heart of the desert, Yazd—like all the towns of the Iranian plateaus—lies at the foot of a mountain range: the Chirkuh, which rises to a height of 13,120 feet.

The production of carpets here was never on any great scale. In the last century the inhabitants of Yazd had their own structure and motifs; later on they brought in designers and weavers from Kerman.

The rug we reproduce is a perfect specimen of Yazd production; one can appreciate the harmonious blending of motifs in the border and in the field.

Pl. 63 TURKOMAN

(Region of Gombad-i-Kabus: Yomud tribe) end of the 19th century
Dimensions: 103 × 60 inches (261 × 153 cm)
Persian knot: 375 knots per sq. inch (580,800 per sq. metre)

16.5 knots per inch width (66 per 10 cm width)
22 knots per inch length (88 per 10 cm length)
Warp: natural beige goat's hair
Single weft: natural grey goat's hair
Pile: wool
5 colours: 2 reds, 1 blue, 1 white, 1 brown

The same octagonal motif (called *salor gul*) assumes two different sizes in this example and covers the whole field of the rug. In the centre of the larger *gul* four compartments can be seen.

The border is made up of three bands of equal size The central one, decorated with twin horns, is called *kochak*, a motif that is very popular with the Turkomans. At each end another border encloses four lozenges known as Yomud *gul*.

TURKESTAN

Pl. 64 BESHIR

(USSR, Turkmenistan) 1970
Dimensions: 54 × 64 inches (264 × 162 cm)
Persian knot: 114 knots per sq. inch (176,000 per sq. metre)
   10 knots per inch width (40 per 10 cm width)
   11 knots per inch length (44 per 10 cm length)
Warp: two strands of natural beige wool
Double weft: grey goat's hair
Pile: two strands of wool of medium thickness, chemically treated to make it glossy and to tone down the brightness of the colours
6 colours: 2 blues, 1 red, 1 orange, 1 white, 1 brownish black

Beshir rugs, from the village of the same name situated in the region of the Amu Darya River, follow one of three designs: the first is composed of a varying number of medallions, from one to five; the second is called *guerat* and has a field covered with stylized plants; and the third, called *ilan*, is reproduced here. The field is filled with coiled curvilinear motifs like formalized serpents.

On the main border, medallions with a central flower alternate with cypress trees. The latter, of conventional appearance on the two bands at the ends, take on the form of crooks at the sides.

Beshir rugs can be distinguished from other Turkoman rugs by the attempt to balance the ground and the pattern harmoniously while retaining, however, a predominance of the latter.

Pl. 65 BUKHARA

(Russian Turkestan) 1950
Dimensions: 115 × 85 inches (292 × 216 cm)
Persian knot: 222 knots per sq. inch (344,000 per sq. metre)
   13 knots per inch width (53 per 10 cm width)
   16.5 knots per inch length (65 per 10 cm length)
Warp: two strands of fine, natural beige wool
Single weft: two strands of fine, natural brown wool
Pile: two strands of fine wool, chemically washed and faded
8 colours: 2 reds, 2 blues, 1 brown, 1 white, 1 yellow, 1 brownish black

Bukhara, a town in Uzbekistan (USSR) with a population of approximately 70,000, has had a particularly

glorious past. In the seventh century, it was already a famous cultural centre. In the tenth century, it fell under Turkish domination; then in the fifteenth century it was taken by the Mongols. After many vicissitudes, it became Russian in 1868.

The town has always had a caravan market for carpets, astrakhan skins and cotton. Like Shiraz in Iran, Bukhara has given its name to a rug without being the centre of its production. The rugs of this region are more properly called "Tekin", a name which is a reminder that their weavers are of the Turkoman race.

Bukhara rugs have been copied very often in other regions, but their beauty has never been equaled. The classic design has remained unaltered. Of recent years the output has dropped; carpets about 6 by 9 feet are particularly uncommon today.

In the example reproduced, we rediscover the classical, typical Turkoman carpet with a design that has not changed for centuries: on a pale rose ground, octagons of consistently rectilinear shape are repeated. One searches in vain for a curved line.

Pl. 66   YOMUD

(Russian Turkestan) *circa* 1910
Dimensions: 84 × 55 inches (213 × 140 cm)
Turkish knot: 144 knots per sq. inch (221,000 per sq. metre)
   9 knots per inch width (34 per 10 cm width)
   16 knots per inch length (65 per 10 cm length)
Warp: two strands of natural beige wool

The Yomud tribe living in the regions of Gassan-Kuli and Tachauz uses colours and designs peculiar to itself, as the rug illustrated shows well. The brownish red ground is crossed by wide bands, whose main decoration consists of large motifs resembling stylized insects. On either side each insect has extended an arm, bearing a small brown cross. These bands are separated by three rows of coiling lines that form bands of unvarying width.

The main border is fairly narrow, and on each side there is a band containing the "running dog" motif used so frequently in the Caucasus. In Turkestan, it is known as a *kilim barmak* (interpreted by some specialists as meaning "the bride's finger").

The colours of this rug are warm, and the brownish red shade is particularly attractive.

Pl. 67   YOMUD ENGSI

(Russian Turkestan), late 19th century
Dimensions: 68 × 58 inches (173 × 148 cm)
Persian knot: 119 knots per sq. inch (181,500 per sq. metre)
   8.5 knots per inch width (33 per 10 cm width)
   14 knots per inch length (55 per 10 cm length)
Warp: two strands of grey goat's hair
Weft: two strands of beige goat's hair
Pile: two strands of wool
12 colours: 2 reds, 1 copper, 3 blues, 2 greens, 1 purplish brown, 1 dark brown, 1 white, 1 gold

This Yomud Engsi or Katchli rug has no *mihrab* and is,

Weft: single strand of natural brown wool
Pile: two strands of wool
8 colours: 1 brownish red, 2 blues, 1 green, 1 orange, 2 browns, 1 white

therefore, not a prayer rug as are most rugs of this type. The four compartments of the field—brown with a slight tinge of purple—are not all of the same size: in two of them there are only three *gul* (small hexagonal motifs) in each row, whereas the other two compartments have five in each row.

The same lack of symmetry is to be observed in the borders. At one end there are three borders, the two narrower ones decorated with stylized birds on a white ground. At the other end there is a wide border, called a *kabyrga* border, as well as another one of equal width with a design of saw-teeth (the so-called fish-bone design) on a blue ground.

The appeal of this rug, whose decoration is rather restrained, lies in the warm shapes and the very attractive pile.

AFGHANISTAN

Pl. 68 AFGHAN

(Aktsha region) 1930
Dimensions: 123 × 93 inches (313 × 236 cm)
Persian knot: 74 knots per sq. inch (114,000 per sq. metre)
    7.5 knots per inch width (30 per 10 cm width)
    9.5 knots per inch length (38 per 10 cm length)
Warp: two strands of brown goat's hair
Double weft: two strands of brown goat's hair
Pile: two strands of rather fine wool

8 colours: 2 reds, 2 blues, 2 browns, 1 orange, 1 white

The whole field of the piece is decorated with *gul* of the Ghazan tribe, which lives in the Aktsha region. These *gul* are octagons of large size, each patterned with four sets of three stems, spouting three leaves, and having wide borders. Between these octagons are diamond-shaped motifs with eight flowers.

The principal border consists of lozenges with inscribed crosses and is framed by two narrow bands decorated with formalized tulips.

Pl. 69   ERSARI-AFGHAN

Circa 1870
Dimensions: 126 × 81 inches (320 × 206 cm)
Persian knot: 66 knots per sq. inch (102,600 per
sq. metre)
   7 knots per inch width (27 per 10 cm width)
   9.5 knots per inch length (38 per 10 cm length)
Warp: two strands of natural greyish brown goat's hair
Weft: two strands of natural greyish brown goat's hair
Pile: two strands of wool
7 colours: 2 copper-reds, 1 copper, 2 blues, 1 brown,
1 white

Most of the copper-red ground of the field is occupied by three lines of contiguous octagons; between these there are *gulli-gul*, a typical Turkoman motif, each containing a star of the Medes, which symbolizes divinity, or the "jewel of Mohammed". This same star appears in each of the squares in the main border. One of the narrow bands near the edge of the rug has a Greek key design on a white ground; some experts call this band a *kilim barmak* (meaning "the bride's finger"). The field is defined by a narrow floral border. The rug is finished at each end by a wide band of striped kilim-weave.

   All the colours of this rug are soft and warm, but it is perhaps the subtle blend of the two shades of copper-red in the ground of the field that is most deserving of our admiration.

INDIA

Pl. 70 KASHMIR

1970
Dimensions: 71 × 48 inches (181 × 123 cm)
Persian knot: 223 knots per sq. inch (345,600 per sq. metre)
    13.5 knots per inch width (54 per 10 cm width)
    16 knots per inch length (64 per 10 cm length)

Warp: five strands of undyed cotton
Double weft: undyed cotton
Pile: two strands of fine wool, chemically washed and faded
12 colours: 3 reds, 3 blues, 2 yellows, 2 beiges, 1 white, 1 brown

The design and colouring of this example are reminiscent of early Agra carpets, which are greatly admired by collectors.

On the field strewn with flowers and animals is a round central motif decorated with floral arabesques and surrounded by a circle of animals and flowers. The floral motifs appear again on the gold ground of the corners.

The red of the main border is that found on early rugs. The decoration of this border, and that of the two narrow surrounding bands of white, is floral.

Although antique in appearance, this carpet is of recent manufacture.

Pl. 71 KASHMIR

1980
Dimensions: 72 × 49.5 inches (183 × 126 cm)
Persian knot: 413 knots per sq. inch (640,000 per sq. metre)
    20 knots per inch width (80 per 10 cm width)
    20 knots per inch length (80 per 10 cm length)
Warp: four strands of unbleached cotton
Weft: two strands of unbleached cotton

Pile: wool and silk
12 colours: 2 reds, 1 black, 2 beiges, 1 green, 1 blue,
1 yellow, 4 browns

Boteh, the princely flowers found on Kashmir shawls in alternate bands, cover the ground of the field in this example. They are encircled by tiny flowers.

The border contains the same motif except at the ends: on either side there is a band of stylized flowers in a series of motifs that resemble little huts.

The harmonious mixture of colours give this carpet a special appeal.

Pl. 72 KASHMIR

1980
Dimensions: 73.5 × 53 inches (187 × 134 cm)
Persian knot: 581 knots per sq. inch (900,000 per sq. metre)
  25 knots per inch width (100 per 10 cm width)
  23 knots per inch length (90 per 10 cm length)
Warp: five groups of two strands of unbleached silk, twisted together
Weft: two strands of unbleached silk
Pile: silk
19 colours: 4 reds, 2 violets, 3 browns, 2 beiges,
5 greens, 3 blues

This composition is inspired by seventeenth-century carpets. The field is almost identical in design with a carpet in the Österreichische Museum für angewandte Kunst, Vienna, which contains a landscape of trees and bushes peopled by pairs of birds.

The main border was inspired by a carpet in the Museum of Fine Arts, Boston; however, contrary to the original, the arabesques here do not terminate in human and animal heads but in floral designs.

Pl. 73 BHADOHI

(Bhadohi region, Varanasi, Uttar Pradesh) 1980
Dimensions: 138 × 99 inches (350 × 252 cm)
Persian knot: 134 knots per sq. inch (208,000 per sq. metre)
  13 knots per inch width (52 per 10 cm width)
  10 knots per inch length (40 per 10 cm length)
Warp: three groups of three strands of unbleached cotton, twisted together
Weft: unbleached cotton
Pile: wool
14 colours: 1 red, 2 pinks, 2 blues, 1 black, 2 greens,
4 browns, 2 beiges

Bhadohi has become an important centre for the production of Indian carpets. The designs used here are based on motifs from the Middle East.

This is a classic example, typical of the Persian influence. The central rosette is perfectly integrated into the graceful scrolls that fill the field between the flowers.

The field is framed by a main border of floral arabesques and enhanced by two narrow floral bands on each side of the main border.

Pl. 74 BHADOHI

(Bhadohi region, Varanasi, Uttar Pradesh) 1980
Dimensions: 125 × 89 inches (318 × 227 cm)
Persian knot: 128 knots per sq. inch (197,600 per sq. metre)
  13 knots per inch width (52 per 10 cm width)
  9.5 knots per inch length (38 per 10 cm length)
Warp: three groups of three strands of unbleached cotton, twisted together
Weft: unbleached cotton
Pile: wool
14 colours: 4 browns, 3 greens, 3 blues, 2 beiges, 2 pinks

Rug production in the region of Bhadohi, near Varanasi, has developed considerably. Previously many rugs were of mediocre quality; however, this has changed. Today Bhadohi rugs are of excellent quality, as this example proves.

The texture is typically Indian, but the design is Persian: a central rosette set in a field of flowers and foliage. The pair of birds in the spandrels adds elegance to the whole.

The main border, enclosed by two floral bands on either side, gives a perfect finishing touch to this harmonious carpet.

CHINA

Pl. 75 NINGXIA

1980
Dimensions: 109 × 69 inches (278 × 176 cm)
Persian knot: 88 knots per sq. inch (136,800 per sq. metre)
   10 knots per inch width (38 per 10 cm width)
   9 knots per inch length (36 per 10 cm length)
Warp: six strands of unbleached cotton
Weft: six strands of unbleached cotton
Pile: wool
8 colours: 2 yellows, 2 mauves, 1 orange, 1 brown, 1 white, 1 red

For some time now, the Ningxia workshops have adopted early classical design of the Beijing (Peking) type and have had recourse to natural dyes of vegetable origin. The charm of this type of carpet lies in the gentle shading of the colours. A lotus flower surrounded by Greek key-frets glows in the centre of the field of this example. The lotus, symbol of purity and fertility, is accompanied on the circumference of the surrounding medallion by four butterflies, emblems of a happy marriage. Flowering branches are scattered over the field. Four medallions, smaller than those in the centre but of similar composition, emphasize the rectangularity of the field; their geometric pattern is repeated in the floral spandrels.

Four bands form the border: the widest is composed of clouds and flowering branches; another has zigzag lines between flower heads shown in half-section. The inner band is ornamented with Greek key-frets, and the outer is undecorated. The overall effect is one of gentleness and serenity.

Pl. 76 SHANGHAI

1980
Diameter: 87 inches (220 cm)
Persian knot: 54 knots per sq. inch (84,000 per sq. metre)
   7 knots per inch width (28 per 10 cm width)
   8 knots per inch length (30 per 10 cm length)
Warp: seven groups of three strands of unbleached cotton, twisted together
Weft: twelve strands of unbleached cotton
Pile: wool
12 colours: 3 browns, 3 greens, 3 pinks, 2 beiges, 1 white

In recent years, the practice of weaving two shoots of weft between each row of knots—for a long time a speciality of Tianjin that is termed "closed back" locally—has been adopted in Shanghai. The term "closed back" signifies that the knotting is tighter than with only a single shoot of weft between each row of knots; the latter type of rug has more loosely spaced knots and is rightly called "open back".

Here, the entire pattern, a type of "aesthetic" design based on French Aubusson carpets, is composed of flowers. Great precision on the part of the craftsman is required when knotting a round carpet, since the number of knots for each row changes constantly. On round carpets, as on rectangular ones, the work is started by setting up the warp threads to run vertically.

The perfect shading obtained with such soft colours is to be admired.

Pl. 77 ÛRÛMQI

1980
Dimensions: 133 × 93 inches (338 × 236 cm)
Persian knot: 81 knots per sq. inch (126,000 per sq. metre)
  9 knots per inch width (36 per 10 cm width)
  9 knots per inch length (35 per 10 cm length)
Warp: twelve strands of unbleached cotton
Weft: twelve strands of unbleached cotton
Pile: wool

8 colours: 2 reds, 2 greens, 1 white, 1 mauve, 1 brown, 1 orange

This rug is reminiscent of early pieces from Hotan and Shache along the Silk Route, with the difference that the medallions no longer enclose pomegranates (as previously) but flowers; however, the flowering stems are those of the pomegranate, which is cultivated in China for its beauty rather than for its fruit. The Chinese see it as the symbol of a propitious influence.

The border is composed of three bands, two of equal width. The outer one is divided: one half has slanted zigzags, and the other a row of ram's horns *(argali)*, signifying man's affinity for things earthly and spiritual. The other two bands are decorated with the flowering branches of the pomegranate.

Soft colours are the key to the harmonious effect achieved here.

Pl. 78 XIZANG (TIBET)

Early 20th century
Dimensions: 50 × 28 inches (128 × 70 cm)
Persian knot: 32 knots per sq. inch (50,000 per sq. metre)
  5 knots per inch width (20 per 10 cm width)
  6 knots per inch length (25 per 10 cm length)
Warp: two strands of unbleached wool
Weft: two strands of unbleached wool
Pile: wool
6 colours: 3 blues, 1 green, 1 red, 1 white

Tibetan rugs are often edged with a cloth of red felt, which can be seen clearly on this example, which is a saddle cover. Here, the felt serves as the lining and is equipped with openings for ease of attachment to the saddle. The size and shape of the rug would correspond to those of the saddle. In order to achieve the correct shape, the two halves of the saddle cover are made separately and then sewn together.

Each side of the rug contains a medallion filled with flowers, probably stylized lotus flowers or peonies. In the eyes of the Buddhist faithful, the former represents purity and creative power *par excellence*, and the latter wealth or love and affection. This repertoire of motifs is carried through on many decorated objects of Chinese porcelain and in scroll-paintings. The medallions are framed with the stems of blossoms.

The border is decorated with large Greek key-frets intersected by flowers.

Pl. 79 BEIJING

Late 19th century
Dimensions: 96 × 61 inches (243 × 154 cm)
Persian knot: 47 knots per sq. inch (72,000 per sq. metre)
  7 knots per inch width (26 per 10 cm width)
  7 knots per inch length (28 per 10 cm length)
Warp: eight strands of unbleached cotton
Weft: six strands of unbleached cotton
Pile: wool
7 colours: 4 blues, 1 white, 1 red, 1 bluish black

In a work written by Gu Yingtai, during the reign of Emperor Tianqi (1621–1627) of the Ming dynasty, the writer states in the twelfth book that embroideries and silks were already cherished during the Han dynasty (206 B.C.–A.D. 220). Dragons, phoenixes, birds and flowers—all the motifs found in painting, silks and rugs of the present day—were woven from that time onwards and are on this carpet. In Chinese folklore, the dragon was a transformed fish, sailing upon stormy waters and half hidden by the clouds. The dragon was often set against the tiger, the king of earthly beasts, who roared as if to defy the invisible power of the spirits. In Chinese ideology, the dragon, far from being the terrible beast of the European Middle Ages, appears as a benevolent being.

On the carpet reproduced here, two dragons emerge from the clouds around a fiery sun or flaming pearl *(jin)* that occupies the centre. Open-jawed, the dragons display whiskers beneath their round eyes; large horns crown their manes, and flames and enormous claws flicker all around their bodies.

The border and, up to a certain point, the composition of the field are reminiscent of an eighteenth-century rug in the collection of the Royal Ontario Museum, Toronto. The border is composed of foaming waves of the sea, arranged symmetrically, with a mountain emerging from the centre. The weaver has displayed great imagination here in the stylization of natural elements.

Pl. 80 BAOTOU

Late 19th century
Dimensions: 77.5 × 49.5 inches (197 × 126 cm)
Persian knot: 52 knots per sq. inch (80,600 per sq. metre)
   8 knots per inch width (31 per 10 cm width)
   6.5 knots per inch length (26 per 10 cm length)
Warp: three strands of fine unbleached cotton
Weft: three or four strands of fine unbleached cotton
Pile: three strands of wool
3 colours: 1 pinkish red, 2 blues

The warp threads of Baotou rugs often run across their width instead of along their length, and the one illustrated is no exception to this peculiarity. The field with a blue ground is filled with lozenges producing a pattern similar to that of a mosaic or a tiled floor. This design—rather appropriate, all in all, for a floor covering such as a carpet—is often found in antique Chinese carpets.

The decoration of the fairly wide main border is a derivation of the swastika motif commonly used in Baotou carpets; immediately surrounding the field, there is a band with a Greek key pattern.

This rug, which employs a very limited range of colours, is typical of those made in Baotou at the end of the last century. The predominant colour is blue (in two shades), and this is relieved by a touch of pinkish red in the flowers.

GLOSSARY

ABRASH
Word used in the carpet trade to denote streaks in the shading of the main colour of a carpet. These streaks, of varying intensities of colour, result from the method of drying dyed wool in the sun. The wool is dried in piles, and the wool at the bottom dries in darker shades than that at the top, not only because it is not exposed to the fading influence of the sun's rays but also because some dye seeps down through the pile of wool.

AESTHETIC DESIGN
Type of design characterized by floral patterns, similar to those on classical French Aubusson carpets.

ARABESQUE
Stylized curving ornament from Islamic art that is derived from the acanthus leaf. The term applies to all complex linear decoration based on curved lines. This type of decoration is especially popular in Persian carpets, where it consists of foliage and flowers curiously intertwined.

ARGALI MOTIF
See: ram's horns.

BARMAK MOTIF
A linear motif, also called a "finger" motif, often found on carpets from Turkestan.

BORDER
The frame of a carpet and an immutable convention of Persian design. It usually consists of a wider middle element—the actual border—with one, two or more narrow guard bands or stripes.

BOTEH MOTIF
A popular motif in Iran and India—where it originated. In its most simplified form its seems to be a serrated leaf. The word comes from the Farsi word for "princely flower". Experts differ on what it represents: a pine, a palm, a cluster of leaves or the sacred flame of Zoroaster.

BOTEH-MIRI MOTIF
A variation of the *boteh* motif, resembling a bush or leaf cluster and characteristic of early Mir rugs.

CARNATION MOTIF
A motif symbolizing happiness and frequently used in the borders of Caucasian and Turkish carpets.

CARTOON
Village weavers were unable to weave the intricate floral and animal designs for large carpets drawn by court painters for fifteenth-century Persian princes. A new technique was therefore evolved, the use of which greatly facilitated the weaving of carpets with very elaborate designs: a designer prepares on paper a preliminary large-scale sketch of the design to be woven; squares (each representing a knot) are then ruled on the sketch by hand, some workers being employed solely for this purpose. The sketch on squared paper is the cartoon, and the method is still in use today.

CLOUD-BAND MOTIF
See: *lingzhi* motif.

DRAGON MOTIF
A fabulous beast used as a motif, especially in Chinese

and Caucasian carpets. The Chinese dragon is benevolent and associated with rain and fertility. It has no wings and resembles a large, snake-bodied lizard with four legs and a fantastic head. Often the dragon is represented pursuing a ball surrounded by flames (commonly described as a "pearl" or *jin*). Both in China and in the Caucasus the dragon is frequently rendered as a mere geometrical form to which a dragon's head is the only clue. The Chinese distinguish four types of dragons: *jiao*, the dragon of the marshes; *li*, the dragon of the sea; *long*, the imperial dragon (with five claws) or the sky dragon *(tianlong)*, a symbol of the emperor and of the power of the spirit; *mang*, the dragon with four claws, the emblem of the princes of the third and fourth ranks.

FIELD
Term for the part of the carpet within the borders.

FRINGE
Decorative border or edging on a carpet, composed of the visible, hanging ends of the warp threads that have been trimmed and knotted.

GROUND (or BACKGROUND)
The general surface of a rug on which the designs are arranged to provide relief for the principal motifs.

GUARD BAND or STRIPE
The narrow band or bands flanking the wider border in the framing of a carpet.

GUL MOTIF
Polygonal Turkoman motif, usually an elongated octa-

gon divided into four, but sometimes lozenge-shaped, formerly used by the nomadic tribes of Afghanistan, Russia and Turkestan as a sort of identifying coat of arms for families and tribes. Also used, though rarely, in the Caucasus. The word *gul* means "rose" or "flower". See also: Salor *gul*, Yomud *gul*.

HAND OF FATIMA MOTIF
A motif used mainly in the Caucasus, symbolizing protection against evil.

JANGALI MOTIF
A colourful floral pattern used on Joshagan rugs; the word *jangali* comes from the Farsi word for "jungle".

JEWEL OF MOHAMMED MOTIF
See: star of Solomon motif.

JIN MOTIF
A circular motif, in the version with flames (usually called the "wishing pearl") a symbol of thunder or of the sun. It represents perfection or protection against evil. See also: dragon motif.

KILIM
An Oriental carpet without a pile that is woven and not knotted. The word is Turkish and denotes a type of flat weave and, by extension, the carpets so woven. In Iran and Central Asia kilims are known as *palas*.

The kilim can be thought of as a stage on the road that led to the development of the knotted rug. It is made according to a technique reminiscent of embroidery. The craftsman weaves under and over the vertical warp threads with a strand of wool threaded through a needle. These horizontal threads serve as the weft and at the same time form the fabric, which is thus devoid of pile. Each shoot of weft reverses the course of the previous one, passing over, instead of under, a given warp thread. Each colour of wool used is taken as far across the loom as the pattern allows. When the colour has to be changed, the warp threads are not fastened together, so a small opening (the characteristic lengthwise slit) can be perceived in the warp at this spot. When the rug is complete, both faces are identical. The perfection of the kilim weave depends on the fineness of the warp and weft threads.

Kilims seem to have originated in the Caucasus, whence they would have been brought by the nomadic tribes who settled in this mountainous region at some indefinite period. Kilims are also produced in southern Anatolia (in the region of Karaman), Iran, the USSR and China, as well as in Tunisia, Yugoslavia, Egypt, Romania and, in a slightly different manner, in India.

KOCHAK MOTIF
See: ram's horn motif.

LATCH-HOOK MOTIF
A motif derived from the swastika and, like it, a symbol of happiness. Frequently used in Caucasian carpets and, in a much rounder form, in Turkoman rugs. The *kufi* design consists of pairs of double latch-hooks alternating with rosettes and lines.

LINGZHI MOTIF
A small, shell-like motif occurring in various forms, some compressed, some elongated. It is thought to represent a single cloud but, in fact, somewhat resembles the conventional Chinese "bank of clouds" motif. The *lingzhi* ("sacred sponge or fungus") is the Chinese symbol of immortality and of the elixir of long life, and is sometimes termed the *chi* or "cloud band" motif.

LOTUS MOTIF
The nelumbo or Indian lotus, as an open flower or bud, used as a motif in Chinese carpets. The lotus is a sacred flower for Buddhists and represents purity, creative power and fertility, as well as being the symbol for summer.

MAHI MOTIF
A floral design found in Persian rugs (also called the "fish in a pond" motif), composed of a rosette surrounded by a garland that is encompassed by two incurved, serrated leaves. The *mahi* motif is widely used in Feraghan rugs and is a variation of the popular *herati* motif, which consists of leaves, flowers with arabesques and lozenges arranged in a regular pattern. There are three versions of the *mahi* or *herati* motif: (a) without a lozenge and found only in rugs from Khorassan, (b) with a lozenge—the most usual version—a classic feature of Feraghan and Mashhad rugs of the second half of the nineteenth century, (c) with a serrated lozenge, woven in the Heriz region at the end of the nineteenth century.

MEDAHIL MOTIF
Farsi term for a reciprocal motif of trefoils or arrow-

heads, used in narrow borders. The motif is widely employed in the Near and Far East.

MEDALLION

A motif, often round or oval, confined to the centre of the field of a rug. Many Persian carpets have a design consisting of a large central medallion, a quarter of which reappears in each corner of the field.

MIHRAB

Design characteristic of prayer rugs and derived from the chamber or prayer niche in a mosque that indicates the direction of Mecca. The upper part of the *mihrab*, called niche in the carpet trade, has sides which slope up to the summit that culminates in a point or arch that must point towards Mecca while the worshipper prays on his rug.

MINAKHANI MOTIF

A pattern consisting of daisies and characteristic of Persian rugs, especially from Varamin. This motif is also found on some rugs from Tabriz and Heriz.

MOSQUE LAMP MOTIF

A realistic or stylized lamp hanging on a chain suspended from the point of the *mihrab*'s arch. Often found on prayer rugs, this motif is reminiscent of similar lamps that hang in mosques.

PALMETTE MOTIF

A motif in the shape of a honeysuckle, probably derived from the flower of the Egyptian or Chinese lotus. The palmette motif is much used in Iran and has embellished Persian carpets since the reign of Shah Abbas the Great (1587–1628); therefore, it is central to the Shah Abbas pattern.

PEONY MOTIF

As a motif on Chinese rugs this flower represents spring and is an emblem of wealth. In southern China the peony is a symbol of love or affection.

PILE

The mass of raised tufts formed by cutting the strands of wool knotted around the warp threads. The pile provides the soft, compact, furry surface of the carpet.

POMEGRANATE MOTIF

For the tribes of eastern Turkestan this fruit symbolizes fertility. In other parts of China and for Buddhists the pomegranate is a symbol of a propitious influence. Both the fruit and the tree are used as motifs to decorate Oriental rugs.

PRAYER RUG

Small Oriental rug used by Moslems to kneel on when saying their daily prayers. Prayer rugs are characteristically decorated with a *mihrab*.

RAM'S HORNS MOTIF

A motif in the shape of a pair of ram's horns, symbolizing affinity with things earthly and spiritual. The Turkoman name for this motif is *kochak* or *argali;* the Caucasian name is *wurma*, and the motif may include the ram's head.

ROSETTE MOTIF

A motif resembling an open rose with the petals arranged in a circle around the centre. The motif is figurative in Persian carpets and highly stylized on Turkoman rugs.

RUNNING-DOG BORDER

Border with a design of running dogs (of Caucasian origin), which is a variation of the Greek key-fret design. The dogs are highly stylized. In the Middle East the dog was the protector of the home and is woven into designs to ward off thieves, illness and evil spirits.

"S" MOTIF

Motif of very early origin in the shape of an "S"; generally assumed to be connected with sun worship and symbolizing light, divinity and wisdom.

SALOR *GUL* MOTIF

A polygonal motif used mainly by the Turkoman Salor tribe. Its outline is in the shape of an irregular octagon. See also: *gul* motif.

SAW-TEETH MOTIF

A design of saw-teeth or zigzag lines with protuberances in the shape of hooks. The lines form serrated lozenges, one inside the other. This motif (also called *ener-dychi* motif) is popular with the Turkoman Yomud and Tekke tribes.

The saw-teeth border motif is a reciprocal motif in which the design resembles the teeth of a saw or serrated leaves. This border is sometimes also called a wine-glass border.

SHAH ABBAS PATTERN

Ruler of the Persian Safavid dynasty from 1587 to 1628, Shah Abbas the Great was a patron of all the arts, but especially of carpet-making. At his capital Isfahan, Shah Abbas set up a factory that produced exceptionally fine hunting and animal carpets, as well as carpets with purely floral designs.

The plant forms in the floral carpets were extremely stylized and included the ancient palmette motif in the centre of the field as the most usual ornament. This type of floral carpet with palmettes is therefore often called the Shah Abbas pattern.

SHEKIRI BORDER

A delicate, lacelike border motif that consists of *boteh* leaves and small flowers. The *shekiri* border is characteristic of Mir rugs.

SIL-I-SULTAN PATTERN

A pattern found on Persian carpets and consisting of roses and other flowers. The term means "shadow of the sultan" and is named after a Qajar prince who was governor of Isfahan in 1890. This design is most commonly found on rugs from Yazd, Tabriz, Isfahan and Khorassan.

SOUMAK

Soumak weaving is similar to tapestry weaving, a technique of flat-weaving that, by extension, is used to designate the carpets so woven. Soumak rugs differ from kilims in that, at the point where the colour is changed, the weft thread is passed under the warp and cut on the reverse side about 1 inch away from the surface of the carpet. The right side of the carpet is smooth, but the reverse presents a tangle of hanging threads.

Soumak rugs are always woven in wool. They originate from the Caucasus, more precisely from Derbent on the Caspian Sea, where manufacture continues today. In recent years the Soumak technique has been used in Iranian Azerbeijan and at Shiraz in Fars province.

SPANDREL
The ornamentally treated corner of a rug between a round field and a rectangular border. Spandrels are filled with figures, scrolls or other motifs, and elements of the central medallion are often repeated in its decoration.

STAR OF SOLOMON MOTIF
An eight-pointed star found in carpets woven by Moslems. The motif (also termed the "jewel of Mohammed" motif) is symbolic of divinity and named after a ring with an eight-pointed diamond which King Solomon was said to possess. The diamond on the ring was called "the star of the Medes", another term for this motif.

SWASTIKA MOTIF
A linear motif of ancient Chinese origin, used throughout the Orient. To Buddhists it represents the heart of Buddha and is thus thought to bring good fortune and happiness.

The *wan*-character meander is a linear Chinese border pattern in which the swastika is continuously repeated.

TARANTULA MOTIF
A motif, popular with nomadic tribes, in the shape of a stylized spider. Harmful insects were not woven into carpets as mere decorative motifs; by incorporating them into his rugs, the weaver hoped to succeed in keeping them away from his house or tent.

TREE OF LIFE MOTIF
This motif of a tree (which may be highly stylized) is often found on prayer rugs because of its religious significance for Islam. It is one of mankind's oldest symbols of life. The *halamdani* pattern consists of elongated hexagons, each containing a tree of life.

WARP
The yarn stretched vertically on a hand-knotted carpet. The knots forming the pile are tied on the warp threads.

WEFT
The yarn that the weaver passes across the width of the carpet between the warp threads. The weft threads maintain the knots of the pile in place.

WINE-GLASS BORDER
A border motif especially popular in the Caucasus. It consists of a stylized glass or goblet arranged in conjunction with a leaf and is therefore also termed the "goblet" border. See also: saw-teeth motif.

YOMUD *GUL* MOTIF
Large, octagonal, lozenge-shaped motif favoured by the Turkoman Yomud tribes, who are related to the Tekke

tribes (which explains the generous use of latch-hooks in old Yomud carpets). See also: *gul* motif.

"Z" MOTIF
Motif in the shape of a "Z", symbolizing light.

ZIGZAG MOTIF
A motif of lines proceeding in sharp turns in alternating directions, frequently used in the Caucasus and Anatolia. The zigzag symbolizes water and eternity. It is often used as a border motif. See also: saw-teeth motif.

This book was set, printed and bound in August 1983 by Benziger AG, Graphische Betriebe, Einsiedeln. Colour photolithography: Atesa-Argraf SA, Geneva.

Design and production: Franz Stadelmann
Map: Marcel Berger
Editorial: Barbara Perroud-Benson

Printed and bound in Switzerland